Herodias

INTERFACES

Series Editor: Barbara Green, O.P.

Herodias

At Home in That Fox's Den

Florence Morgan Gillman

A Michael Glazier Book

LITURGICAL PRESS
Collegeville, Minnesota

www.litpress.org

A Michael Glazier Book published by the Liturgical Press.

Cover design by Ann Blattner. Watercolor by Ethel Boyle.

The Scripture quotations, unless otherwise indicated, are from the New Revised Standard Version Bible © 1989 by the Division of Christian Education of the National Council of Churches of Christ in the U.S.A. Used by permission. All rights reserved.

1	2	3	4	5	6	7	8

Library of Congress Cataloging-in-Publication Data

Gillman, Florence Morgan.
   Herodias : at home in that fox's den / Florence Morgan Gillman.
      p. cm. — (Interfaces)
   "A Michael Glazier book."
   Includes bibliographical references.
   ISBN 0-8146-5108-9 (alk. paper)
   1. Herodias. 2. Bible. N.T.—Biography. I. Title. II. Interfaces (Collegeville, Minn.)

BS2452.H47 G55 2003
225.9'2—dc92

2002029845

CONTENTS

PREFACE

The book you hold in your hand is one of six volumes in a new set. This series, called INTERFACES, is a curriculum and scholarly adventure, a creative opportunity in teaching and learning, presented at this moment in the long story of how the Bible has been studied, interpreted, and appropriated.

The INTERFACES project was prompted by a number of experiences that you, perhaps, share. When I first taught undergraduates the college had just received a substantial grant from the National Endowment for the Humanities, and one of the recurring courses designed within the grant was called Great Figures in Pursuit of Excellence. Three courses would be taught, each centering on a figure from some academic discipline or other, with a common seminar section to provide occasion for some integration. Some triads were more successful than others, as you might imagine. But the opportunity to concentrate on a single individual—whether historical or literary—to team teach, to make links to another pair of figures, and to learn new things about other disciplines was stimulating and fun for all involved. A second experience that gave rise to the present series came at the same time, connected also with undergraduates. It was my frequent experience to have Roman Catholic students feel quite put out about taking "more" biblical studies since, as they confidently affirmed, they had already been there many times and done it all. That was, of course, not true; as we well know, there is always more to learn. And often those who felt most informed were the least likely to take on new information when offered it.

A stimulus as primary as my experience with students was the familiarity of listening to friends and colleagues at professional meetings talking about the research that excites us most. I often wondered: Do her undergraduate students know about this? Or how does he bring these ideas—clearly so energizing to him—into the college classroom? Perhaps some of us have felt bored with classes that seem wholly unrelated to research, that rehash the same familiar material repeatedly. Hence the idea for this series of books to bring to the fore and combine some of our research interest with our teaching and learning. Accordingly, this series is not so much about creating texts *for* student audiences, but rather about *sharing* our scholarly passions with them. Because these volumes are intended each as a piece of original scholarship they are geared to be stimulating to both students and established scholars, perhaps resulting in some fruitful collaborative learning adventures.

The series also developed from a widely-shared sense that all academic fields are expanding and exploding, and that to contemplate "covering" even a testament (let alone the whole Bible or Western monotheistic religions) needs to be abandoned in favor of something with greater depth. At the same time the links between our fields are becoming increasingly obvious as well, and we glimpse exciting possibilities for ways of working that will draw together academic realms that once seemed separate. Finally, the spark of enthusiasm that almost always ignites when I mention to colleagues and students the idea of single figures in combination—interfacing—encourages me that this is an idea worth trying.

And so with the leadership and help of Liturgical Press Academic Editor Linda Maloney, as well as with the encouragement and support of Managing Editor Mark Twomey, the series has begun to take shape.

Each volume in the INTERFACES series focuses clearly on a biblical character (or perhaps a pair of them). The characters are in some cases powerful (King Saul, Pontius Pilate) and familiar (John the Baptist, Joseph) though in other cases they will strike many as minor and little-known (the Cannibal Mothers, Herodias). In any case, each of them has been chosen to open up a set of worlds for consideration. The named (or unnamed) character interfaces with his or her historical-cultural world and its many issues, with other characters from biblical literature; each character has drawn forth the creativity of the author, who has taken on the challenge of engaging many readers. The books are specifically designed for college students (though we think suitable for some graduate work as well), planned to provide young adults with relevant information and at a level of critical sophistication that matches the rest of the undergraduate curriculum. In fact, the expectation is that what students are learning in other classes on historiography, literary theory, and cultural anthropology will find an echo in these books, each of which is explicit about at least two relevant methodologies. It is surely the case that biblical studies is in a methodology-conscious moment, and the INTERFACES series embraces it enthusiastically. Our hope is for students (and teachers) to continue to see the relationship between their best questions and their most valuable insights, between how they approach texts and what they find there. The volumes go well beyond familiar paraphrase of narratives to ask questions that are relevant in our era. At the same time the series authors have each dealt with the notion of the Bible as Scripture in a way that is comfortable for them. None of the books is preachy or hortatory, and yet the self-implicating aspects of working with the revelatory text are handled frankly. The assumption is, again, that college can be a good time for students to rethink their beliefs and assumptions, and they need to do so in good company.

The INTERFACES volumes are not substitutes for the Bible. In every case they are to be read with the text. Quoting has been kept to a minimum for that very reason. The volumes, when used in a classroom setting, are accompanied by a companion volume, *From Earth's Creation to John's Revelation: The INTERFACES Biblical Storyline Companion,* which provides a quick, straightforward overview of the whole storyline into which the characters under special study fit. Web links will also be available through the Liturgical Press website: www.litpress.org.

The series challenge—for publisher, writers, teachers, and students— is to combine the volumes creatively, to "interface" them well so that the vast potential of the biblical text continues to unfold for all of us. The first six volumes: in Old Testament/Hebrew Bible featuring Saul, the Cannibal Mothers, and Joseph; in New Testament focusing on John the Baptist, Herodias, and Pontius Pilate, offer a foretaste of other volumes currently in preparation. It has been a pleasure, and a richly informative privilege, to work with the authors of these first volumes as well as the series consultants: Carleen Mandolfo for Hebrew Bible and Catherine Murphy for New Testament. It is the hope of all of us that you will find the series useful and stimulating for your own teaching and learning.

Barbara Green, O.P.
INTERFACES Series Editor
June 29, 2002
Berkeley, California

ACKNOWLEDGMENTS

Herodias and her daughter, Salome, have been on my mind (and desk!) for some time. After giving papers entitled "Political Wives in the New Testament" at the International Congress on the Bible and Religion, Melbourne, Australia, in July 1992, "The Synoptic Portrayal of Herodias" at the Catholic Biblical Association of America at the University of San Diego in August 1994, and "Salome: A Mere Pawn in the Baptist's Death?" in the Women in the Biblical World Section of the Society of Biblical Literature, New Orleans, in November 1996, I expanded the material into this book.

My research has been supported by various faculty research grants and sabbatical time from the University of San Diego, for which I am most appreciative. My gratitude also extends to the Steber Endowment for the Steber Professorship it has awarded me, enabling the completion of this text. It has been my pleasure to have personally met Mrs. Frances Steber. I sincerely thank her for the generous endowment she and her late husband, Clarence Steber, have given to promote the research of the faculty of Theology and Religious Studies at the University of San Diego.

Throughout the work on this book and especially during its final editing I received a great deal of help from my husband, John. His painstaking work has contributed much to the smooth reading of the text, and I am very grateful. He, and our daughter Annie, are ever my joy and support. Another voice of loving encouragement who always inspires me is my mother, Ann Morgan. This book is dedicated to these three special people in my life.

ABBREVIATIONS

AB	The Anchor Bible
ABD	*Anchor Bible Dictionary,* David Noel Freedman, ed.
Ant.	Flavius Josephus, *Antiquities of the Jews*
Antip	*Antipas*
Apion	Flavius Josephus, *Against Apion*
BAR	*Biblical Archaeology Review*
BETL	Bibliotheca ephemeridum theologicarum lovaniensium
BZNW	Beihefte zur Zeitschrift für die neutestamentliche Wissenschaft
CBQ	*Catholic Biblical Quarterly*
CSCT	Columbia Studies in the Classical Tradition
HE	Eusebius, *Historia Ecclesiastica*
HTR	*Harvard Theological Review*
ICC	International Critical Commentary
JBL	*Journal of Biblical Literature*
JSOT.SS	Journal for the Study of the Old Testament: Supplement Series
JW	Flavius Josephus, *The Jewish War*
KJV	*Authorized (King James) Version*
LCL	Loeb Classical Library
Life	Flavius Josephus, *The Life*
LXX	Septuagint
MSSNTS	Monograph Series, Society for New Testament Studies
NAB	*New American Bible*
NEAEHL	*The New Encyclopedia of Archaeological Excavation in the Holy Land,* E. Stern, ed.
NJBC	*The New Jerome Biblical Commentary*
NRSV	*New Revised Standard Version*
NT	New Testament
OGIS	*Orientis graeci inscriptiones selectae,* W. Dittenberger, ed.
OT	Old Testament
VAgr	*Vita* of Agrippa

INTRODUCTION

In the Lair of Antipas

*"Herod was a foxy man. We sometimes meet with these foxy people.
They want to go to heaven, but they like the road to hell.
They will sing a hymn to Jesus, but a good roaring song they
like also. They will give a guinea to the church,
but how many guineas are spent on their own lust.
Thus they try to dodge between God and Satan."* [1]

The subtitle of this book is drawn from some name-calling done by Jesus. When told that Herod Antipas wanted to kill him, Jesus retorted:

> "Go and tell that fox for me, 'Listen, I am casting out demons and per-
> forming cures today and tomorrow, and on the third day I finish my
> work. Yet today, tomorrow and the next day I must be on my way, be-
> cause it is impossible for a prophet to be killed outside of Jerusalem.'"
> (Luke 13:32-33) [2]

Jesus knew that the tetrarch would not hesitate to murder a prophet. [3] Antipas had already executed John the Baptist.

The remarks of Jesus betray an assessment of Antipas, for to dub him a fox, *alōpex,* was pejorative; it implied he was sly and crafty, a base character whose position was gained not by power and dignity but by deceitful

---

[1] Joseph S. Exell, *The Biblical Illustrator: St. Mark* (New York: Fleming H. Revell Co., n.d.) 243.

[2] All biblical quotations are from the NRSV unless otherwise noted.

[3] In musing on the bravery it takes to call a reigning king a fox, William Barclay, *The Gospel of Luke* (Philadelphia: Westminster, rev. ed. 1975) 186, tells a story about Bishop Hugh Latimer (1485–1555) preaching in Westminster Abbey when Henry VIII was in the congregation: "In the pulpit Latimer soliloquised, 'Latimer! Latimer! Latimer! Be careful what you say. The king of England is here!' Then he went on, 'Latimer! Latimer! Latimer! Be careful what you say. The King of Kings is here.'"

maneuvering. Jesus makes it clear that he intended to escape the cunning of Antipas by moving out of his jurisdiction over Galilee and Peraea as he made his way to Jerusalem. Jesus was destined to be killed not by Antipas, but in Jerusalem, the traditional killer of prophets.[4]

The Women in That Fox's Den

While this book will say much about Antipas and his role in the death of the Baptist, "that fox" is not our central interest. The focus is rather on a woman who was effectively caged in his den due to patriarchal convention. Yet Mark and Matthew say that she ultimately snared him via intrigue, thus leaving her own impact on the events of her time. This woman is Herodias, Antipas' niece and second wife. With her story one must also tell of Salome, her daughter and accomplice, as well as various other women in both Antipas' and Herodias' family history. These include Herodias' mother, Berenice, her grandmother, Salome, and her predecessor, the first wife of Antipas, who also brilliantly outsmarted him.

These women are a subset of a larger, powerful group of women, namely those who were born or married into the Hasmonean and Herodian families. Much is known about these aristocratic females, thanks in large part to the writings of the ancient historian Josephus. The place in history of four of these Hasmonean/Herodian women is also dramatically under-scored by their mention in the New Testament and the direct link they had with the story of Christian origins.

Hasmonean/Herodian Women in the New Testament

The four Hasmonean/Herodian women of the NT are Herodias and her daughter (Mark 6:17-29; Matt 14:3-12; Luke 3:19-20), and Herodias' nieces, Drusilla (Acts 24:24-26) and Berenice (Acts 25:13–26:32). Each of these women is reported to have interacted with, been consulted about, or known of John the Baptist or Paul. They must also have heard about Jesus (see Mark 6:14//Matt 14:1//Luke 9:7-9; Luke 23:8-12).

These four women form a subset, not only among Jewish aristocratic women, but also among all NT women. From the NT perspective they com-

---

[4] Jesus surely knew that, while many prophets had died in Jerusalem, others like John the Baptist had been put to death elsewhere. G. B. Caird, *Saint Luke,* Pelican New Testament Commentaries (New York: Penguin, 1963) 173, suggests that Jesus was implying that Antipas had no right to usurp the position accorded to Jerusalem over many centuries as *the* killer of God's messengers.

prise a group of wealthy Jewish political wives, sisters, and daughters who were individually either opposed to, indifferent toward, or unpersuaded by the preaching of the Baptist, the testimony of Paul, or what they may have heard about the teaching of Jesus. Of these aristocratic Jewish female rejectors of Jesus, John, or Paul, as I would categorize them, Herodias and Salome are the most famous, due to their role in the Gospels.

Why Study Aristocratic Women Who Rejected John the Baptist, Jesus, and Paul?

This text has grown out of my interest in the individuals who were part of the drama of Christianity's earliest history, especially the females.[5] The women of the period of Christian origins have been closely studied in the past few decades. This is due to the raised consciousness that the females in the NT have been neglected in reconstructing the history of the earliest churches, their stories patriarchally suppressed liturgically and homiletically. What little has been told was often misogynistically presented. The more recent emphasis in retrieving women's history, however, has been on women *sympathetic* to Jesus or the early Christians. This is understandable since much of the impetus for late-twentieth-century scholarly focus on women in early Christianity arose out of justice issues of gender discrimination and inequity in churches today. But scholarship on NT women has also been driven by the inadequacy of past historical syntheses.

Since the 1970s, when the quest for the historical women of the NT era claimed a place in academic discussion, much has been published on the earliest Christian women. Ironically, however, those NT women about whom the most is known, those for whom the greatest literary and archaeological source material is extant, namely the Herodian women, have been least examined. They have commanded less attention because they were *not sympathetic* to nascent Christianity, and one would hardly study them in hopes of finding role models for ending the injustice toward women in Christianity today.

Why, then, should we pursue the story of such a woman and others like her? My agenda is historical and exegetical. Intended for university biblical studies courses, this text is about history and the passing on of traditions in literature. Books that teach about Christian origins ought to offer as complete a reconstruction as possible, yet that has not happened with

---

[5] See my *Women Who Knew Paul*, Zacchaeus Studies: New Testament Series (Collegeville: The Liturgical Press, 1992).

Herodias. She is a notable figure in any overview of earliest Christianity, since the NT credits her with mistress-minding the death of John the Baptist. However, little is generally said about her and other Herodian women in textbooks on biblical studies and early church history.[6]

In working toward closing that gap this study assumes that just as biblical scholarship understands that the women sympathetic to early Christianity were given androcentric portrayals in the NT traditions and documents, so, too, Herodias entered into ancient documentation with a male slant imposed on narration concerning her.

Herodias the Prism

Studying Herodias reminds me of looking through a prism. Through her, as if seeing rays of light converging from and being refracted toward different angles, one can learn a great deal about the NT era, the Jewish and Greco-Roman world, and how male authors such as the evangelists and Josephus edited material about women. Even though Herodias is a minor character in both NT and ancient history one can experience her as a window into the ancient world.

This book is thus a study of Herodias as its subject in her own right and as a means for a reader to enter her world. It is also a case study about how her story has been passed on. It offers (1) a reconstruction of elements of NT history neglected widely in university-level textbooks, that is, a biographical treatment of Herodias, and (2) an exegetical analysis of material about her in the Synoptic Gospels following the standard approaches of literary criticism.

In accord with the majority of Synoptic Gospel commentators, my assumptions are those of the Two Source Theory, i.e., the priority of Mark. According to this approach, when Matthew and Luke wrote their gospels, independently of each other, each used much of Mark and added to it non-Markan material, the so-called Q source. Matthew and Luke also included material proper to themselves.

It is necessary that chapters three through six of this book be read with a synopsis, a parallel version of the Synoptic Gospel texts of Mark 6:17-29//Matt 14:3-12//Luke 3:19-20. These texts are provided in Appendix B.

---

[6] For the general history of Jewish women in Greco-Roman Palestine see Tal Ilan, *Jewish Women in Greco-Roman Palestine: An Inquiry into Image and Status* (Peabody, Mass.: Hendrickson, 1995) 2–21, which gives a thorough overview of research since the late nineteenth century.

Females at the Mercy of Males', Ink.

"I would rather live with a lion and a dragon than live with an evil woman. A woman's wickedness changes her appearance, and darkens her face like that of a bear. Her husband sits among the neighbors, and he cannot help sighing bitterly."

(Sir 25:16-18)

As both a biography of Herodias and an exegetical analysis of the NT passages about her, this book is threaded with feminist concerns. I have sought to portray Herodias as she lived in a matrix of other females, but not to the exclusion of males. This counterbalances studies in which the Herodian family is discussed in terms of the men, with women mentioned as appendages. A feminist perspective will also be noticed in the questions asked and suspicions expressed concerning the literary treatment of females by male writers. A question pervading this investigation concerns how male writers may have stylized Herodias and other women for their own purposes. Behind such feminist redactional analysis is, of course, the quest for the historical Herodias and her female relatives and friends. Admittedly, that quest is difficult and will be successful only to a degree.

At the beginning of chapters and under some subheadings I have included quotations from biblical books, the writings of church fathers, and sermons of late-nineteenth/early-twentieth-century male preachers. Many of these passages reflect misogynistic perspectives, hardly genuine wisdom, and are shocking to an educated modern person. These quotations serve as a counterweight or foil to the feminist concerns of my text. Most of these generalizing statements, for example the one cited immediately above, can be read as the voice of a patriarchal Herodian male, such as Antipas, who faults women like Herodias for his unhappy situation. How different the outcome—so he might ponder—had he only remembered the misogynistic "wisdom" typically taught to males of his era. A few of my quotations reflect genuine, non-sexist wisdom. I will leave it to the reader to determine where I have, tongue in cheek, cited misogynistic advice and where I have quoted genuine wisdom (yes, a puzzle!).

From the Quill of Josephus

The fame accorded for the last two thousand years to Herodias and to her even more renowned daughter, Salome, is due to their presence in the NT. Yet most literary data about them comes from other first-century C.E.

sources, *The Jewish War* (hereafter *JW*) and *The Antiquities of the Jews* (hereafter *Ant.*), both by Flavius Josephus. A brief introduction to Josephus and his writings is thus in order.[7]

A descendant of the Hasmoneans born into a priestly lineage, Josephus (37–ca.100 C.E.) was a Jewish military leader and then a collaborator with the Romans during the Jewish War of 66–70. He later became an historian. In his writings Josephus drew upon numerous sources, written and oral. These included a life of Herod the Great written by Nicolaus of Damascus,[8] various versions of the biblical text, traditional midrash, handbooks of Greek historians, and Roman decrees. In a recent study Daniel Schwartz concludes that among Josephus' written sources was a document concerning the life of Herodias' brother, Agrippa I, and one on her second husband, Antipas. The author of the latter showed a notable interest in Antipas' wives.[9] Schwartz labels these *VAgr* (*Vita* of Agrippa) and *Antip* (Antipas) respectively. In regard to some passages that will be cited in our study, Schwartz assigns *Ant.* 18.143-46, 151-58, 161-237 to *VAgrip;* he ascribes *Ant.* 18.147-50, 159-60, 238-55 and *JW* 2.178-83 to *Antip*.

Scholars assume that Josephus had much oral tradition about his Hasmonean ancestors and their Herodian rivals and successors. Josephus himself says that he consulted with Agrippa II, who was Herodias' nephew and the son of Agrippa I. I will suggest later that in the years he was writing in Rome Josephus also had access to Queen Berenice, the sister of Agrippa II.

The Jewish War, the earliest and most famous of Josephus' works, was first written, according to him, in his ancestral language, presumably Aramaic. His purpose was to send a narrative to the barbarians of Parthia and Babylonia to warn them against making the mistake the Jews had in rebelling against Rome. Josephus translated and revised the original Aramaic—no longer extant—into Greek, with heavy reliance upon assistants. The first six books in Greek are generally thought to have been published near the end of the reign of Vespasian, thus about 79 C.E., although some would place their release just a year or two later under the reign of

---

[7] See Louis H. Feldman, "Josephus," *ABD* 3:981–98. Concerning Josephus as the most significant non-biblical writer with respect to NT interpretation see Steve Mason, *Josephus and the New Testament* (Peabody, Mass.: Hendrickson, 1992).

[8] Nicolaus (b. ca. 64 B.C.E.) was a well-educated Greek writer who served as advisor and court historian for Herod the Great. He had previously taught the children of Marc Antony and Cleopatra.

[9] Daniel R. Schwartz, *Agrippa I. The Last King of Judea,* Texte und Studien zum Antiken Judentum 23 (Tübingen: Mohr, 1990).

Titus; the seventh and final book was probably composed near the end of the first century.[10]

The purpose of this Greek version of *JW*, directed to a Greco-Roman audience, was not to offer Roman propaganda as might be expected. Rather it was to influence readers to view the Jews positively by understanding that their war against Rome was caused by only a few troublemakers. Josephus implies that the Roman victory was not due to Roman gods; it came from the Jews' own God, who had used the Romans to punish the Jewish rebels.

The Antiquities of the Jews, structured in twenty books, was written ten years or more after *JW,* or about 90 C.E. Josephus intended this to be an overview of the history of the Jewish people from the creation, as recounted in the Bible, up to the period of the Jewish War. Like *JW,* though much longer, *Ant.* was written apologetically; it is intended to counter misinformation about the Jews by showing the antiquity and nobility of their traditions.

Josephus' treatment of first-century C.E. events in *Ant.* overlaps in some sections with the early chapters of *JW,* although with various alterations. His testimony in *Ant.* concerning NT events and persons, namely Jesus, James the brother of Jesus, and John the Baptist, is significant as a source independent of the NT. This is certainly the case as regards the differing data provided by the NT and *Ant.* about the death of John the Baptist.[11]

When working with *JW* and *Ant.* it is important to note that there is uncertainty about the reliability of the Greek text.[12] The oldest extant manuscripts, apart from one earlier papyrus fragment, date from the eleventh century. Since other documents both before and after the eleventh century quote information that differs from the known texts, it could be that there were versions of Josephus differing from the surviving manuscripts. Many of the variant readings may have entered the manuscripts due to paraphrasing and legendary insertions. For example, there is an eleventh-century

[10] On the dating of *JW* see Shaye J. D. Cohen, *Josephus in Galilee and Rome: His Vita and Development as a Historian,* Columbia Studies in the Classical Tradition VIII (Leiden: Brill, 1979) 84–90.

[11] Much scholarship judges that Josephus' works were preserved in their entirety due to his references to Jesus, John, and James; Christians saved what Jews regarded as the writings of a traitor. In the case of the reference to Jesus (*Ant.* 18.63-64), the so-called *Testimonium Flavianum,* many suspect the text contains alterations made by a Christian interpolator. Josephus' passage about the Baptist (*Ant.* 18.116-19), however, is generally judged to be authentic.

[12] The standard critical editions of the writings of Josephus in Greek with English translation relied upon here are the nine-volume set published in the Loeb Classical Library.

translation, actually a paraphrase, of *JW* into old Russian, known as Slavonic Josephus, that has material on John the Baptist and Herodias not in the Greek text and thus not in modern editions of Josephus. This data (treated in our epilogue) is generally held to be a late Christian embellishment of the text of Josephus.

Josephus and Women

As we draw upon Josephus to reconstruct the life and times of Herodias, the absence of other ancient sources with which to compare what he says about her and other women is problematic. How far can Josephus be trusted in what he says women did, and in the motives and qualities he attributes to them? Tal Ilan has provided an analysis of Josephus' attitudes toward some Hasmonean/Herodian women.[13] Her starting point is to note that Josephus was heavily dependent upon the writing of Nicolaus of Damascus for information about the period of Herod the Great. Ilan observes that the description Josephus took from Nicolaus concerning the royal women in the Hasmonean and Herodian courts, extending from the period of Shelamzion Alexandra to Salome, Herodias' grandmother, offers a stridently negative perspective on royal women. Salome in particular is characterized as an evil *femme fatale*. The portrayals of these women reflect the writer's opinion that "behind every calamity lurks a woman, or as the French would have it—*cherchez la femme*."[14]

Because such negativity is without precedent in the writings of Josephus about earlier periods of Jewish history, and disappears after he exhausts Nicolaus as a source, Ilan theorizes that the negativity comes from Nicolaus. She does not propose this in order to acquit Josephus and blame someone else for the misogynism in his narrative. Rather it is to recognize that the very powerful women of the Hasmonean and Herodian dynasties in his writings are dramatic literary creations of Nicolaus' imagination.[15] Josephus himself is seen by Ilan as an historian who, while evidently misogynistic, in contrast mostly ignored women and only mentioned them in his narrative when he had to. She bases this assessment of Josephus' attitude toward

---

[13] Tal Ilan, "Josephus and Nicolaus on Women," in Peter Schäfer, ed., *Geschichte—Tradition—Reflexion. Festschrift für Martin Hengel zum 70. Geburtstag. Band I: Judentum* (Tübingen: Mohr, 1996) 221–62.

[14] Ibid. 222.

[15] Ibid. 223. See also eadem, "The Attraction of Aristocratic Women to Pharisaism during the Second Temple Period," *HTR* 88 (1995) 1–33, at 6: ". . . Nicolaus was much more interested than Josephus in the role women played in politics, and was usually quick to blame them for most calamities, political and otherwise, that befell Herod's court."

women on texts in which he is not using sources such as Nicolaus or the Bible.[16]

Ilan's analysis underscores that the negative portrayal of the various Hasmonean and Herodian women in Josephus cannot be read uncritically as historical. If these accounts cannot be accepted at face value, neither can their counterparts in other ancient historiography, including Roman writings. The latter likewise often attribute to royal women certain stock charges and major roles in affecting events via intrigue. This is equally true with respect to the Gospel descriptions of Herodias and her daughter and raises serious questions regarding the redaction of their story by the evangelists.

Because misogynism permeates the material Josephus took from Nicolaus, runs through his own lack of interest in women's lives, and must also be assumed in the hateful caricatures of royal women in Roman sources and in the NT, it must be stressed that what we compile about Herodias and other women here speaks of them primarily on the *literary* level of our sources. This means that these documents must be approached with suspicion insofar as we would like to know the characters historically. Herein will also be found many difficulties throughout this book, for layers of misogynist and otherwise androcentric male redaction have buried to a great extent the historical individuals we would really like to find.

The Game Plan: Mine and Theirs

This study of the life of Herodias uses a chronological, biographical format. Chapters One and Two cover her early life and her two marriages. Chapters Three and Four then focus upon the best-known event in Herodias' life, her role in the execution of John the Baptist. The Synoptic Gospel texts are surveyed and compared with each other. Since Mark's gospel is presumed to be the source from which Matthew and Luke took their information, Matthew's and Luke's texts are each compared with Mark.

Methodologically this leads in Chapter Five to an analysis of the Matthean and Lukan redactions of Mark. It is logical after that to finally focus just on Mark in Chapter Six. There we ask questions of source criticism (Where did Mark get his story about Herodias and the Baptist?), form criticism (What type of story is this, and therefore how does it function for Mark and the reader?), and redaction criticism (Did Mark edit or even create the story, and if so, for what purposes?). Chapter Seven completes the biographical frame of the book by looking at Herodias and Salome after

---

[16] "Josephus and Nicolaus," 231–32.

the death of the Baptist. A brief epilogue treats their "existence" via their great fame even after their own deaths.

In sum, this book is about Herodias, with much about her daughter and other Herodian women, as people of their world and times, as participants in the history of early Christianity, as examples of females in texts by Josephus and the synoptic authors. In the drama of their lives Herodias and Salome played parts that have become unforgettable, roles in which they are portrayed as having made decisions out of love and decisions out of hate. They are said to have killed a prophet, or better put, to have manipulated a fox called Antipas into killing a man of God for them. What game were they playing, and by whose rules did they abide?

CHAPTER ONE

Passages:
The Road to Herodian Womanhood

*"The strife of the proud leads to bloodshed,
and their abuse is grievous to hear."*

(Sir 27:15)

Herodias was the child of two first cousins, Berenice and Aristobulus. Berenice's parents were Salome, Herod the Great's powerful sister, and Costobarus. Costobarus was an Idumean; Salome and Herod, although of mixed Idumean and Nabatean descent, were generally considered Idumeans as well.[1] Aristobulus was Herod's son by his Hasmonean wife Mariamme I. Herodias was thus partly Hasmonean, but predominantly Idumean.

Berenice and Aristobulus married about 17 B.C.E., after Aristobulus and his brother, Alexander, returned to Judea following five years of study in Rome. The marriage of Herodias' parents may have been unhappy, for Berenice's mother, Salome, was the main accuser of Aristobulus' mother, Mariamme I, when the latter was put to death by Herod in 29 B.C.E. This situation mirrors the domestic struggles between the Hasmonean and Idumean branches of Herod's family that permeated his rule and household.

---

[1] Salome and Herod came from an aristocratic Idumean family whose forebears had converted to Judaism during the reign of John Hyrcanus I, when he forced the non-Jewish population of Idumea to be circumcised in 129 B.C.E. Their mother, Cypros, came from a distinguished Arab, probably Nabatean, family; their father, Antipater, was an adviser to Hyrcanus II and became the overseer of Judea in 47 B.C.E. Antipater, in turn, appointed Herod governor of Galilee. In 40 B.C.E. the Roman Senate named Herod King of Judea. On Herod see especially Lee I. Levine, "Herod the Great," *ABD* 3:161–69; Peter Richardson, *Herod: King of the Jews and Friend of the Romans* (Columbia: University of South Carolina Press, 1996).

1

One wonders if there was friendship between Berenice and her mother, considering that Salome had divorced Berenice's father, Costobarus, and allegedly encouraged Herod to execute him (*Ant.* 15.253-66). After Berenice married, she and her mother were certainly allies. Josephus comments on the situation twice:

> . . . Salome, who was bitterly hostile to the sons of Mariamme, would not even allow her own daughter who was married to Aristobulus . . . to show him any wifely affection; instead she persuaded her to report to her anything which he might say to her privately, and whenever there was friction between them, as sometimes happens, she would sow great distrust in her daughter. In this way Salome learned of everything that passed between them and also made her daughter hostile to the youth. (*Ant.* 16.200-202)

> Aristobulus himself alienated Salome, his own mother-in-law . . . for he was continually upbraiding his wife for her low origin, saying that he had married a woman of the people. . . . Salome's daughter reported this, with tears, to her mother; she added that Alexander and Aristobulus had threatened, when they came to the throne, to set the mothers of their other brothers to work at the loom along with the slave-girls, and to make the princes themselves village clerks. . . . Salome, unable to control her indignation, reported the whole to Herod; as she was accusing her own son-in-law, her evidence carried very great weight. (*JW* 1.478-80)

The problems were exacerbated by Glaphyra, the wife of Aristobulus' brother, Alexander. As daughter of the king of Cappadocia she taunted Salome and Herod's various wives about their low birth. Toward Berenice in particular Glaphyra's attitude was insolent, for she "regarded with indignation" that Berenice ranked equally with her (*Ant.* 16.193). This led Aristobulus to make the comparison to Berenice that while he had married her, "a woman of the people," Alexander had married a princess (*JW* 1.478). According to Josephus it also caused Salome to spread the rumor that Herod was "smitten with love for [his daughter-in-law] Glaphyra and that his passion was difficult to assuage" (*Ant.* 16.206). This angered Alexander and worsened his and his brother's relationship with Herod.

Developments such as these were among the many that precipitated the execution by strangling of Aristobulus and Alexander in 7 B.C.E. The evidence that convinced Herod that they were plotting patricide was supplied not only by their half-brother, Antipater, and Herod's brother, Pheroras, but by Salome (*JW* 1.545-46). One wonders again about Berenice, by that event widowed. Was she still friendly with her mother, unquestioning about this woman who had had her father killed and now had colluded in her husband's death as well? Or had Berenice been either a passive or willing accomplice in implicating Aristobulus?

Since the data above concerning Salome's intrigues came to Josephus via Nicolaus it cannot be known whether the malicious, conspiratorial literary character of Salome was historically so. While many scholars think she was indeed monstrous, others are not certain, because Nicolaus is known to have been at personal enmity with her.[2] There is, however, no doubt that Salome was a major power broker during Herod's regime and within their family. What her relationship with Berenice was like is a matter for speculation, although the two women clearly functioned as allies throughout their lives.

Daughter of Hasmoneans and Idumeans

Due to the death of Aristobulus in 7, his and Berenice's children were born no later than 7–6 B.C.E. They had three sons, Herod (of Chalcis), Agrippa (I), and Aristobulus, and two daughters, Herodias and Mariamme, presumably all born in Judea. This order of their names, as found in *JW* 1.552, suggests that Herodias was older than her sister. However, in another text concerning their betrothal the order is reversed.

Some estimate that Herodias was born shortly before her father's death, i.e., between 9 and 7 B.C.E.[3] It is more probable, however, that she was born earlier and was older than Agrippa and Aristobulus, for in 6 B.C.E., when Herod the Great arranged marriages for the children of Berenice and Aristobulus, he did not include their sons Agrippa and Aristobulus, who must have been too young.[4] If Herodias was older than Agrippa her birthdate was before 11–10, when he is certain to have been born (see *Ant.* 19.350). It appears, therefore, that Herodias was born between 16 and 12 B.C.E. Her siblings Herod and Mariamme, betrothed when she was, must have been born during the same years, but the birth order of the three remains uncertain.

Herodias, with her one-fourth Hasmonean descent as granddaughter of Mariamme I, had a legitimizing factor in her claim to be royalty that few

---

[2] On Nicolaus and Salome see Tal Ilan, "Josephus and Nicolaus on Women," in Peter Schäfer, ed., *Geschichte—Tradition—Reflexion. Festschrift für Martin Hengel zum 70. Geburtstag. Band I: Judentum* (Tübingen: Mohr, 1996) 252–59.

[3] Ben Witherington, "Herodias," *ABD* 3:174–76, at 174.

[4] Daniel R. Schwartz, *Agrippa I. The Last King of Judea.* Texte und Studien zum Antiken Judentum 23 (Tübingen: Mohr, 1990) 39–40.

Herodians had, including her other three illustrious, but predominantly Idumean, grandparents.[5] In her descent from Hasmonean dynastic women Herodias followed upon some very strong characters, such as the wives (names unknown) of Simon Maccabeus and John Hyrcanus I, as well as Queen Shelamzion (Salome) Alexandra and her granddaughter, Alexandra. The latter's daughter was Mariamme I, Herodias' grandmother. These women had variously undergone captivity, torture, political restrictions, and physical constraints. Joseph Sievers concludes that they were "ready, willing, and able to shape the world around them, to take risks, and often to assume painful responsibilities."[6] Sievers notes that the extraordinariness of these women, mainly known from events that took place after they were widowed or separated, shows that in each case they were "the remaining female members of the dynasty [who] had an opportunity and a need to take their destiny and that of their family into their own hands—and a sizable number did so with great vigor and considerable skill."[7]

Herodias' Hasmonean grandmother, Mariamme, was Herod's second wife. While Herod may indeed have loved her, it was also to his political advantage to marry into the Hasmoneans. Whether Mariamme wanted to enter this marriage is impossible to determine. After 35 B.C.E., when Herod killed her brother, she hated him with increasing intensity. Her outspokenness contributed to her downfall. Herod, alleging that Mariamme had committed adultery and had prepared love potions and drugs to harm him, ordered her executed in 29 B.C.E. Her death, however, did not end her presence in Herod's life. The thought of her haunted him, and Mariamme's sons, Alexander and Aristobulus, never forgave him.

One of the most powerful persons around Herod had always been his sister, Salome. This Idumean grandmother of Herodias had found ways to survive shifting family liaisons and widespread, almost incessant political

---

[5] Grace H. Macurdy, *Vassal-Queens and Some Contemporary Women in the Roman Empire* (Baltimore: Johns Hopkins University Press, 1937) 78, has suggested that if Herodias was validated as royal by one grandparent she was energized by descent from the other three. Macurdy contends that Herodias inherited on both her maternal and paternal sides certain dominant Herodian traits (which Macurdy saw in Salome and her brothers, Herod and Pheroras) such as "unbounded energy and ambition, recklessness in abandonment to the passion of love, and fierceness in vengeance on those who baulked or resisted her." But this assessment must be questioned since it relies on dramatized historiographical descriptions of the Herodians by Nicolaus as taken over by Josephus.

[6] Joseph Sievers, "The Role of Women in the Hasmonean Dynasty," in Louis Feldman and Gohei Hata, eds., *Josephus, the Bible and History* (Detroit: Wayne State University Press, 1989) 132–46, at 144. This study does not treat Hasmonean women after Mariamme I.

[7] Ibid. 145.

intrigue. Salome outlived her siblings and numerous family members by many years. She was alive well into the adulthood and first marriage of Herodias. Herodias' observation of how Salome, and her own mother, Berenice, negotiated loyalties in order to survive offered her vivid models for navigating the roiling waters into which she was born.

Indeed, this daughter of Hasmoneans and Idumeans, this Herodian princess, empowered by the stories of her ancestors and those who raised her, became no less a survivor and shaper of her own destiny. She, too, learned to play the game of survival and advancement in her birth family. She eventually became a skilled participant, especially in matches that pitted her first against a black ram and later against a fox and a prophet.

After Grandfather Executed Father

After Herod ordered Aristobulus and Alexander put to death in 7 B.C.E. he himself brought up their children "very carefully" (*Ant.* 17.12). To what extent Herodias lived in Herod's presence during the three years between her father's death and Herod's own, however, is not evident. In his final years Herod often stayed in Jericho. Herodias must have spent time there in Herod's palace complex, with its lavish swimming pool.[8] The betrothal event of the children of Aristobulus and Alexander, described twice by Josephus, probably took place at that Jericho palace. One version is presented as a speech he places in the mouth of Herod:

[8] In the valley of Jericho, at the mouth of the Wadi Qelt, a site now called Tulul Abu el-ʿAlayiq, the Hasmoneans had built a winter palace complex. Due to their construction of a network of aqueducts, much land could be cultivated in the area and the waters could also support winter homes for the upper classes of Jerusalem. The Hasmoneans protected the area with a chain of fortresses erected in the hills around the valley. In the early years of the Roman takeover Marc Antony gave Jericho, including this winter palace section of it, to Cleopatra as a gift. She ruled it from 35–30 B.C.E., and during that time leased it to Herod the Great. Following her suicide in 30 B.C.E., Octavian restored Jericho to Judean rule. During his reign Herod developed the Hasmonean palace area, which had been badly damaged by an earthquake in 31 B.C.E., into three palaces. These multiple buildings of the complex may also be understood as a single unit that Herod had constructed in three stages. It included luxurious rooms, mosaic-carpeted halls, terraces, a Roman-style bathhouse, a large swimming pool and gardens. In this pool in 35 B.C.E. Herodias' great uncle, Aristobulus III, was drowned during a party, at Herod's order (*JW* 1.435-37; *Ant.* 15.50-61). This brother of Mariamme I was the last Hasmonean contender for Herod's throne and popular with the crowds in his role as high priest. On these excavations see Ehud Netzer, "Tulul Abu el-ʿAlayiq," *NEAEHL* 2, 682–91; Inge Nielsen, *Hellenistic Palaces. Tradition and Revival.* Studies in Hellenistic Civilization 5 (Aarhus: Aarhus University Press, 1994) 155–63; 193–200.

. . . Herod, one day, assembled his relatives and friends, set the young children before them, and said, with tears in his eyes: "I have been bereaved by some evil genius of the sires of these infants, but pity for the orphans and nature alike commend them to my care. If I have been the most unfortunate of fathers, I will try at any rate to prove myself a more considerate grandfather and to leave their tutelage, after my death, to those most dear to me. . . . To your son [name unknown], Antipater,[9] I betroth the daughter of Aristobulus [Mariamme]; so may you [Antipater] become a father to this orphan girl. Her sister [Herodias] my own Herod shall take, for on his mother's side [Mariamme II] he is grandson of a high priest. Let then effect be given to my wishes, and let no friend of mine frustrate them. And I pray to God to bless these unions, to the benefit of my realm and of my descendants, and to look with serener eyes upon these children here than those with which he beheld their fathers." Having thus spoken he gave way to tears and joined the children's hands, and then fondly embracing one after the other dismissed the assembly. (*JW* 1.556-59)

Josephus' second and shorter summary of this event is in narrative form. It tells not only of the betrothals of Mariamme and Herodias, but also of that of their brother, Herod:

. . . On one occasion he [Herod] presented the young children to a gathering of his friends, and after bewailing the fortune of his sons, prayed that no such fate might befall their children and that by improvement in virtue and concern for righteousness they would repay him for bringing them up. He also promised in marriage, when they should reach the proper age . . . the daughter of Antipater to Aristobulus' son [Herod of Chalcis], and he designated one daughter of Aristobulus [Mariamme] to marry the son of Antipater, and the other daughter of Aristobulus [Herodias] to marry his own son Herod, who had been born to him by the daughter of the high priest, for it is an ancestral custom of ours to have several wives at the same time. (*Ant.* 17.12-14)

The final explanatory clause in *Ant.* 17.14 may imply that the Herod to whom Herodias was betrothed was already married.

These plans were made by Herod shortly before his death, "out of pity for the orphaned state of the children and to induce Antipater [their uncle and Herod's heir-apparent at the time] to feel kindly toward them because

---

[9] Antipater was a son of Herod the Great by his first wife, Doris.

of the marriage connexion" (*Ant.* 17.15-16). For political reasons, however, Antipater was dissatisfied and persuaded Herod to make certain changes (*JW* 1.562-66; *Ant.* 17.17-18), including betrothing himself, instead of his son, to Herodias' sister, Mariamme (*Ant.* 17.18). Herodias' betrothal, however, was not altered. In arrangements also made by Antipater, Berenice was married shortly after Aristobulus' execution to Antipater's uncle, Theudion.

Although Antipater had influenced all these arrangements he mattered little in the long run, for Herod soon turned against him. Antipater was accused of a plot to kill Herod with poison obtained from Egypt by various conspirators, including Theudion. Herod ordered Antipater's death just five days before his own demise. Whether Theudion was punished or Berenice was implicated with her new husband in the conspiracy is not known.

A Roman Period:
Friends, Romans, and Country (Wo)men

It appears that shortly before the death of Herod, Agrippa I was living in Rome. While *Ant.* 18.143 mentions only that Agrippa was there, Daniel Schwartz comments that "by the time Herod died, in 4 B.C.E., Berenice had already taken Agrippa and his siblings to Rome."[10] Although the same passage also comments that there his mother "ranked high among her [Roman] friends," it is not evident when Berenice went to Rome. Had she gone with Agrippa before Herod's death, and with or without Theudion? Or, did she go after Herod's death, for example when Salome is said to have taken her family to Rome? And were Berenice's other children besides Agrippa with her in Rome?

A question of great interest here is whether Herodias herself was in Rome. Schwartz's assumption that Berenice would have taken all her children with her is probably accurate. It appears that in *Ant.* 18.143 Josephus drew upon *VAgr*, which centered on Agrippa's life. Mention of the rest of the family was germane only if it advanced the narrative about Agrippa. By saying he was in Rome with his mother, *VAgr* does not therefore exclude the other siblings being there as well.[11] Further evidence that Berenice and her children were in the imperial city, if not just before Herod's death then shortly thereafter, is Josephus' note that Salome took her "children" (*JW* 2.15), that is, her "family" (*Ant.* 17.220), to Rome after

---

[10] Schwartz, *Agrippa I*, 40.

[11] The presence of Agrippa's older brother, Herod of Chalcis, and his education in the same circles as Agrippa and Claudius is confirmed by Claudius' expression of friendship for this Herod and his son in *Ant.* 20.13.

Herod died.[12] Hence it is reasonable to assume that Herodias lived in Rome with her grandmother and mother beginning no later than Salome's 4 B.C.E. journey.

The reason Salome and her family went to Rome may not have meant much to the young Herodias, but it would affect her future political status. It also ironically foreshadowed a later trip to the imperial court that she herself would make. Salome's journey was triggered by matters following Herod's death. His numerous wills, complicated by codicils, resulted in the succession being contested in particular by Archelaus and Antipas, his sons by Malthace the Samaritan. Archelaus, the elder of the two, was designated as Herod's successor in his final will. Acting as if he had already been confirmed on the throne, he had proven through his handling of an uprising that his rule would be brutal. Antipas had also been named Herod's successor, but in a previous will. Since no one could officially take power without the approval of Augustus, both Archelaus and Antipas, with separate parties, set out for Rome. Josephus states that Salome accompanied Archelaus and ostensibly meant to help him in his bid for the throne, but in reality she intended to work against him (*JW* 2.15; *Ant.* 17.220). When Antipas also sailed for Italy "he was encouraged by Salome's promises to believe that he would rule" (*Ant.* 17.224; see also *JW* 2.20).

Once in Rome, all of Antipas' relatives went over to his side "not out of good will to him, but because of their hatred of Archelaus" (*Ant.* 17.227; see also *JW* 2.22-23). Salome and her collaborators sent an indictment of Archelaus to the emperor. In an interview with Augustus involving all the disputants Antipas' chief proponent was Salome's son, Antipater, a skillful speaker. Nevertheless, the matter was decided in favor of Archelaus. Augustus awarded neither of Herod's sons the title of king, however. He gave Archelaus the role of ethnarch over half the territory Herod had ruled, essentially Judea, Samaria, and Idumea. The rest was divided between Antipas and Philip, another of Herod's sons who had followed his brothers to Rome to assert his own claim. These two were called tetrarchs. Antipas received Peraea and Galilee; Philip was given Batanaea, Trachonitis, and Auranitis.

Although no resentment is reported on the part of Antipas at his demoted status, Josephus asserts that it bothered Herodias in later years when she was his wife. She would then, perhaps spurred on by memories of her grandmother, demand another trip to plead his case in Rome. The result was even worse than demotion. But that is getting ahead of our story.

---

[12] In addition to her daughter Berenice, and a son (name unknown) also by her second husband, Costobarus, Salome had an older son, Antipater, by her first husband and another daughter by either her first or second husband (*JW* 1.566).

Salome, while not absolutely triumphant through Antipas, made out reasonably well for herself in Rome. She was recognized by Augustus as Herod's fourth main inheritor. Along with confirming what Herod had bequeathed to her, the cities of Jamnia (Yavneh), Azotus (Ashdod), and the new city of Phasaelis in the Jordan valley, as well as five hundred thousand pieces of coined silver, the emperor also gave her the royal palace in Ascalon (Ashkelon) (*JW* 2.98; *Ant.* 17.321).[13] Her estates, over which she would have been considered the ruler, were technically placed under the jurisdiction of Archelaus (*JW* 2.98).[14]

In assessing how Augustus resolved the dispute among Herod's heirs we should note that he treated the Herodians as a dynasty. Bo Reicke comments:

> Herod I [the Great] was an upstart; always a vassal, he was not granted a successor of royal rank. Nevertheless, with Augustus' consent, the government of Palestine remained in the hands of Herod's family. For Herod himself and his host of children the idea of a dynasty had become a firm conviction. The primary reason the offspring of the Idumean usurper strove so zealously to gain the royal inheritance was that their father had convinced them that royal blood flowed in their veins.[15]

At the same time it was in Rome's best interest to maintain the appearance that Herod's descendants, albeit weakened, still ruled.[16]

By the time Salome took her family to Rome in 4 B.C.E. Herodias must have been nearing ten, an age at which marriage was just a few years away. With Berenice's family considered royalty and potential rulers,

---

[13] Herod the Great had bestowed numerous honors on the seaport of Ascalon since it was his birthplace, the city where his grandfather, Herod of Ascalon, had been a *hierodule* (temple slave) in the temple of Apollo (so Julius Africanus as quoted by Eusebius, *HE* 1.6). During his reign Herod built a palace there for Augustus, which was the palace the emperor in turn bestowed upon Salome.

[14] Richardson, *Herod,* 40, points out that while it was rather unusual in Jewish practice for a female to share in inheritance distribution, these arrangements for Salome "might be explained either as a result of Roman and Hellenistic practices or as an exception to the Jewish practices, predicated on Herod's closeness to Salome and her closeness to the Emperor's family."

[15] Bo Reicke, *The New Testament Era* (Philadelphia: Fortress, 1968) 114.

[16] See John H. Hayes and Sara R. Mandell, *The Jewish People in Classical Antiquity* (Louisville: Westminster John Knox, 1998) 150: "In accord with the traditional Roman methods of governing those under Rome's hegemony, whereby client rulers governed, thus sparing Rome expense and difficulty, Augustus decided that it was best for the sons of Herod, rather than Rome directly, to deal with the anarchic conditions."

Herodias and her other children would have entered easily into Rome's prestigious circles.

In the Diaspora but Not of It

While it is certain that the Herodian family socialized with the Roman aristocracy, we may wonder about their relationship with the Jews in Rome. As members of the ruling elite of the Jewish homeland, to what extent did they mingle with the large Roman Jewish populace, estimated to have been as high as fifty thousand in the period of Augustus?[17]

The presence of Aristobulus' children must have been popular with the Roman Jews, for they had supported him and Alexander. This was reflected in an incident shortly after Herod's death when a charlatan arrived in Rome claiming to be Alexander, saying that both he and Aristobulus, supposedly then in Cyprus, had been secretly spared by Herod's executioners. Roman Jews in great number enthusiastically poured out to see him until he was discovered to be a pretender (*Ant.* 17.330-38). If this episode took place about 3 B.C.E. as some date it,[18] one wonders why Salome and Berenice are not mentioned by Josephus as the obvious persons to test the imposter's identity. Perhaps the incident happened a year or two earlier, before their arrival in Rome. In any case, the likelihood that the Jews of Rome would have felt kindly toward Aristobulus' children should probably be seen merely as enthusiasm for their Hasmonean descent from Mariamme I, i.e., a longing for the good old days of Hasmonean rule. The Roman Jews were hardly enthusiastic about the Herodians in general, as evidenced during the negotiations over Herod's will. Rome's Jews at that time sent eight thousand people to join a party of envoys from Judea to ask Augustus to end the rule of the Herodians (*Ant.* 17.300). It is probable, therefore, that Herodias, Agrippa, and their siblings, despite some popular enthusiasm for their *Hasmonean* descent, would not have been encouraged by their *Herodian* grandmother and mother to interact with Rome's non-aristocratic Jewish population.

As for Jewish observance and synagogue connections,[19] it is doubtful that Salome and Berenice from their Idumean perspective would have even

---

[17] On Rome's Jewish community see Harry J. Leon, *The Jews of Ancient Rome* (Peabody, Mass.: Hendrikson, updated edition 1995).

[18] Schwartz, *Agrippa I*, 43.

[19] See Leon, *Jews of Ancient Rome*, 140–41, concerning the Synagogue of the Agrippesians in Rome's Transtibertine district. While Agrippa I or his son, Agrippa II, may have been the source of the synagogue's name, it may rather have honored Marcus Vipsanius

promoted the Jewishness of their family, particularly when living in Rome. However, Jewish proselytism was quite energetic in the imperial city, one result being that among the Roman aristocracy there was a degree of fascination with Judaism. That, ironically, may have prodded the Herodians to be somewhat observant "when in Rome."

The Ladies of the Club

Salome and Berenice wove an intricate web of friendships with influential Romans over the years. When Herodias was in Rome, from about 4 B.C.E. until probably 1 or 2 C.E., after which she was living in her first marriage in Judea, her social life would have been determined by her maternal connections with, above all, Livia and Antonia.

Livia (57 B.C.E.–29 C.E.)[20] was one of the most powerful political figures in first-century Rome. The daughter of a nobleman, Livia Drusilla was first married to Tiberius Claudius Nero in about 43 B.C.E. They had two sons, the future emperor Tiberius and Drusus (the Elder). When Livia was six months pregnant with Drusus she was divorced, because her compliant husband had acquiesced to Augustus (Octavian), who wanted her himself. Augustus in turn divorced his first wife, Scribonia, on the day their only child, Julia Major, was born. He married Livia that very same day, 17 January 38 B.C.E. Livia's first husband attended the wedding and even gave away the bride. Livia lived with Augustus, apparently faithfully and devotedly, for fifty years. None of their children survived beyond birth.

Augustus adopted both of Livia's sons, whose interests she was concerned to promote. She became alienated from Tiberius by meddling in his affairs, but when he became emperor in 14 C.E. her political prestige increased. She was then given the title of Julia Augusta. Livia's influence was exercised especially through the patronage she bestowed upon numerous clients, with whom she met in her house on the Palatine hill. She wielded power for almost seventy years until her death in 29 C.E.

Livia's friendship with Salome spanned the years of Augustus' rule (31 B.C.E.–14 C.E.), until the death of Salome in 10 C.E. How the two women became linked is not certain. Since Salome's brother, Herod, was a client king of Augustus and Livia, gifts were exchanged on numerous occasions.

Agrippa, the son-in-law of Augustus, who is known to have shown favor to the Jews, and for whom Agrippa I himself was probably named.

[20] On Livia see, e.g., Matthew Bunson, *A Dictionary of the Roman Empire* (New York: Oxford University Press, 1991) 241–42; Diana E. E. Kleiner and Susan B. Matheson, eds., *I, Claudia. Women in Ancient Rome* (New Haven: Yale University Art Gallery, 1996) passim.

For example, for the celebration of Herod's new city of Caesarea Maritima (ca. 12 B.C.E.) Augustus sent equipment for the games, and Livia "sent many of her greatest treasures from Rome" (*Ant.* 16.139). Salome and Herod, in turn, each made bequests in their wills to both Augustus and Livia.

Livia's friendship with Salome was a notable factor in two matters. In about 7 B.C.E. Salome wanted to marry Syllaeus the Arab as her third husband. He was the procurator of Abodas, king of Arabia. Herod, however, had sworn that he would not be on good terms with Salome unless she married Alexas, one of his friends. Salome turned to Livia to intercede on her behalf. Livia, however, sided with Herod, and persuaded Salome to marry Alexas lest open enmity be declared between herself and Herod. Salome took Livia's advice "both because she was the wife of Caesar and because on other occasions she would give her very helpful counsel" (*JW* 17.10).

The friendship between Salome and Livia also figured in some events a few years later, when it was exploited by Antipater. In an attempt to frame Salome so that Herod would execute her (*JW* 1.641-46; *Ant.* 17.134-41), Antipater had letters purported to have been written by Salome sent to Herod from Rome through a Jewish slave of Livia named Acme. Indicating she had found the letters among Livia's papers, Acme said she was a sympathizer of Herod and was forwarding the letters so that he could read Salome's cruel remarks about him. The letters, however, were exposed as forgeries and it was revealed that Antipater had bribed Acme to send them. Herod then wrote to Augustus concerning the fraud, and this resulted in the execution of Acme (*JW* 1.661). The episode contributed to Herod's decision to execute Antipater as well shortly thereafter.

Not long after these events Herod himself died and Salome and her family went to Rome to dispute his will. Good relations existed then and were maintained between Livia and Salome. This is apparent since Salome was well rewarded in Augustus' administration of Herod's will, and Salome's daughter Berenice and various of her children stayed on in the imperial city for some years. The friendship between Livia and Salome, as well as the patron-client bond between them, would have woven together many individuals from their respective families. Herodias thus would have known people both powerful and controversial. The tension and intrigue in the imperial family were paralleled only by those in her own. This is apparent throughout Livia's story. Before looking at more of that, however, we must also discuss the friendship between Berenice and Antonia.

Antonia (the Younger) (36 B.C.E.–37 C.E.), the daughter of Marc Antony and Octavia, was Augustus' sister. She married Drusus, Livia's second son and the younger brother of Tiberius. Before Drusus died in 9 B.C.E. they had several children, including Claudius, Germanicus, and Livia Julia (Livilla). Although the *Lex de maritandis ordinibus* of the period stipulated that widows had to remarry, Augustus allowed Antonia to remain single. As Livia's closest friend, Antonia also got along with Tiberius. Antonia's son Claudius and her grandson, Gaius (Caligula) each became emperor. Antonia and Berenice, according to Josephus, were "deeply attached" (*Ant.* 18.165); Berenice ranked high among her friends, and Agrippa and his siblings shared in that friendship.

Livia and Antonia were the major figures in the social circles that welcomed Salome, Berenice, and their family. It is interesting to envision the young Herodias in this company. Her brothers, like other young princes from throughout the empire, were there to be educated and to form friendships and bonds of patronage with the future power brokers of the Roman elite. The younger ladies of the imperial set, both Herodian and Roman, were likewise forming patron-client bonds. Who were the younger Roman females with whom Herodias might have socialized? Among them most likely were the children of Julia Major.[21]

Julia Major (39 B.C.E.–14 C.E.) was Augustus' only child, the daughter of Scribonia, whom he had divorced the day Julia was born in order to marry Livia. Julia's first husband, Marcellus, died in 23 B.C.E. She then married Marcus Vipsanius Agrippa as his third wife and had five children by him. A year after his death in 12 B.C.E. Julia was compelled by Augustus to marry her stepbrother Tiberius, Livia's son. Augustus had ordered him to divorce his wife, Vipsania, in order to marry Julia.

Unable to bear the loss of his beloved Vipsania, and filled with hatred, Tiberius left Julia in 6 B.C.E. and moved to Rhodes. Julia comforted herself by taking many lovers and boasting about them. Her actions, which flouted her father's widely touted moral propaganda, aroused fierce hostility from him. A terrible scandal erupted. Julia had violated the model of behavior for royal women promoted by Augustus and set before the public by Livia. Above all, her promiscuity caused great problems for Augustus since it made uncertain the hitherto unquestioned paternity of her five children, Augustus' only grandchildren and potential heirs. Although the sexual liberty Julia had adopted was hardly different from what her father had

---

[21] On the Ara Pacis Augustae, the Altar of Augustan Peace, which was made in Rome between 13 and 9 B.C.E., there are idealized portraits of Augustus' family, including Livia, Julia and her children, and foreign royal children in their household. See Elaine Fantham et al., *Women in the Classical World. Image and Text* (New York: Oxford University Press, 1994) 294–95.

enjoyed in his younger years, Augustus denounced her publicly. In 2 B.C.E. he exiled her to the island of Pandateria in the Bay of Naples. Tiberius then divorced Julia, but also wrote from Rhodes to try (unsuccessfully) to lighten her punishment. Julia's mother, Scribonia, chose to accompany her to Pandateria.

Julia Major was a contemporary of Berenice. Her five children, Gaius Caesar, Lucius Caesar, Julia, Vipsania Agrippina (the Elder), and Agrippa Postumus formed part of the society Herodias and her siblings moved within. Julia Major's daughter, Julia, about the same age as Herodias, was exiled to the island of Trimerium in 8 C.E. for the same behavior that had led to her mother's earlier banishment.[22]

Livia, whose great concern was the advancement of Tiberius, and for whom, therefore, Julia's three sons stood in the way as heirs to the throne, was accused of the murders of both Lucius (d. 2 C.E.) and Gaius (d. 4 C.E.) and of being instrumental in the exile of Agrippa Postumus and his eventual murder in 14 C.E. after the death of Augustus. In Julia's daughter, Vipsania Agrippina, Livia and Tiberius were to have their most bitter opponent. Agrippina, like her sister Julia, was almost an exact contemporary of Herodias.

Agrippina (ca. 14 B.C.E.–33 C.E.) was happily married to Germanicus, the brother of Tiberius, by whom she had nine children. Like Germanicus she valued republican ideals, which did not sit well with Tiberius and Livia. Considered proud and imperious, she nevertheless became popular with the army after accompanying Germanicus on a military campaign. When he died under mysterious circumstances in 19 C.E. she openly blamed Tiberius and Livia. In 29 she, too, was exiled to Pandateria, where her mother had earlier been sent. Before banishing Agrippina, Tiberius personally flogged her, putting out one of her eyes. On Pandateria Agrippina died by starving herself.

These later events of Agrippina's life would not have been known to the young Herodias when she was in Rome, just as Agrippina would have had no clue as to what lay ahead for Herodias. Assuming Herodias' Roman sojourn was from 4 B.C.E. to 1 or 2 C.E., she would have socialized with Agrippina and Julia when she and they were entering their marriageable and childbearing years. Together they were aristocratic young women learning the rules of survival in their families and in their wider political milieu. Salome, Livia, Berenice, Antonia, and Julia Major would have

---

[22] She lived there for about twenty years, aided by secret support from Livia. Not only was Julia exiled, but a child born to her in exile was not allowed to live. Augustus also ordered her house in Rome destroyed.

been Herodias' chief mentors on how to navigate the murky political, familial, and especially marital waters of her elite existence.

Return to Judea:
Over the Sea to Grandmother's Palace

In the scenario sketched above it has been estimated that Herodias was in Rome from 4 B.C.E. until 1 or 2 C.E. The *terminus a quo* is determined by the date of Herod's death and the contestation of his will, which took Salome and her family there. The *terminus ad quem* is gauged by the probable date of Herodias' first marriage and the assumption that she returned to Judea just before entering into it. Related to this is the question of how long Salome stayed in Rome.

Josephus says almost nothing about Salome after the events in Rome in 4 B.C.E. He does, however, date her death to the procuratorship of Marcus Ambivulus (*Ant.* 18.31), which implies that she died in Judea between 9 and 12 C.E. Apart from this *terminus ad quem,* indicating the latest date Salome could have returned to Judea, it is more likely that she went back relatively soon after Herod's will was settled in order to assert authority over the cities she had inherited. She may have done this not only in her own interest but also to channel income to Berenice and her children in Rome. Maybe Herodias returned to Judea then with Salome, in which case her Roman sojourn would have been shorter than estimated here. However, since Berenice evidently stayed in Rome with Agrippa for the years of his education it is plausible that she kept her other children with her until they were mature. Herodias, who must have been marriageable by 1 or 2 C.E., probably returned to Judea at that point. A likely scenario would be that her mother sent her to Salome, who could arrange for her marriage based upon the betrothal Herod had sealed many years earlier.

First Marriage: The Ram Was Black

> *"Birds roost with their own kind. . . ."*
>
> (Sir 27:9)

Herodias' first husband was Herod II, her half-uncle. Perhaps not his first wife, she may have married him in 1 or 2 C.E. This dating derives from the estimation that she was born between 16 and 12 and married near age sixteen, although Jewish custom of the period reflects a wide range of age for a woman's first marriage. Since Herodias had been young when betrothed it is likely her marriage took place as soon as she was mature. Also, the time for her to marry may have been influenced by the Roman elite circles in which her family moved; for them the widespread practice was early marriage for women. Concerning this custom Gillian Clark gives this instructive example:

> . . . The pressure of mortality was the underlying reason for early marriage. Tullia, Cicero's cherished daughter, was engaged at 12, and married at 16, to an excellent young man. She was widowed at 22, remarried at 23, divorced at 28; married again at 29, divorced at 33— and dead, soon after childbirth, at 34. The evidence of inscriptions shows that she was not untypical.[23]

Herod II (born ca. 23 B.C.E.) was the son of Herod the Great and Mariamme II, daughter of the high priest Simon Boethus. As grandson of a high priest he is called Herod Boethus by some commentators, although nothing attests he was so named. Other issues also surround his name since Matt 14:3 and Mark 6:17 call him Philip. Some have posited that both Josephus and the Gospels are correct and therefore call him Herod Philip. But Herod the Great is not known to have had a son by that name. What seems more probable is that Herod II and Philip were two different people and that Mark, followed by Matthew, confused Herod II with the husband of Herodias' daughter, Philip the tetrarch.[24]

Herodias and Herod II had a daughter named Salome. Her birth may have been as early as 3 C.E., but it may also have been as late as 20.[25] Since she was probably named for her mother's grandmother, she is likely to have been born after Salome's death between 9 and 12.

With the death of her grandmother, Herodias must have lost her chief mentor. She would go on in life to emulate Salome in striking ways. Salome's death probably also affected Herodias economically. Salome left a will, which Josephus describes twice. *Jewish War* 2.167 states: "Salome . . . at her death bequeathed her toparchy to Julia [Livia], the wife of Augustus, together with Jamnia and the palm groves of Phaesalis." *Antiquities* 18.31 says that Salome left to Livia "Jamnia and its territory, together with Phaesalis, which lay in the plain, and Archelais, where palms

---

[23] Gillian Clark, "Roman Women," *Greece and Rome* 28 (1981) 193–212, at 201.

[24] See Gary A. Herion, "Herod Philip," *ABD* 3:160–61. The theory advanced by Nikos Kokkinos, "Which Salome Did Aristobulus Marry?" *Palestine Exploration Quarterly* 118 (1986) 33–50, at 42, that Herodias was married to both Herod II and then Philip before Antipas is contradicted by the text of *Ant.* 18.109-11, 136.

[25] On the date of her birth see below, p. 119.

are planted in very great numbers and the dates are of the highest quality." Josephus gives no other provisions from the will. Not all of Salome's territories, however, were deeded to Livia. Azotus and her palace at Ascalon are missing. This could be an oversight on the part of Josephus, but it could also be that Salome bequeathed them to Herodias or to Berenice. Herodias' possession of either Azotus or the palace at Ascalon, or both, might be evidenced by the fact that she was later known to have possessions independently of her second husband and to have lived with her first husband at or near the coast.

That Herodias and Herod II lived in or near a harbor city is evident in Josephus' narrative when Herod's half-brother, Herod Antipas, visited them before he set sail for Rome (*Ant.* 18.109-11). While Azotus or Ascalon may have been their residence, Caesarea Maritima is a possibility as well. Caesarea was a likely port for Antipas to depart from. Also, Herod the Great had built a magnificent palace there, where his son Herod II and Herodias may have resided.[26]

Herod II and Herodias apparently lived out of the public eye, and probably less sumptuously than other Herodians like Antipas. Their existence as private citizens is traceable to events just before the death of Herod the Great, when Herod II's mother, Mariamme II, was accused of collaborating with Antipater, Berenice, and Theudion to poison Herod. The king's punishment for Mariamme's audacity fell upon her son; he was struck out of his father's will (*JW* 1.600). Herod the Great also divorced Mariamme and took away the high priesthood from her father, Boethus (*Ant.* 17.78).

Why had Herodias married into this disgraced branch of her family? The betrothal made by her grandfather before the disgrace involving Mariamme had obviously remained in force despite Herod II's disinheritance. And, marrying young, like the other women of her family, Herodias would have had no say in the arrangements made years earlier for her by the males of her family. Later in life, however, she did manage to gain some determination over her marital fortunes.

---

[26] The dramatically located and now excavated Promontory Palace in Caesarea, perched on a rock mass jutting into the sea, is thought to be Herod's palace. See Barbara Burrell, Kathryn Gleason, and Ehud Netzer, "Uncovering Herod's Seaside Palace," *BAR* 19/3 (1993) 50–57, 76. These authors infer from Acts 23:35, with its statement that Paul (in ca. 60 C.E.) was kept under guard in Caesarea in "Herod's headquarters," i.e., in his *praetorium,* that the palace had become the official residence of the Roman governors of Judea. They do not speculate, however, how soon after Judea was organized as a Roman province in 6 C.E. the palace takeover by the governors happened. It is possible that members of the Herodian family such as Herod II and Herodias were allowed by the Romans to use it.

It is impossible to know what Herodias felt about her first marriage. Her husband's apparent lack of political ambition and lower economic status compared with many other Herodians may explain her eventual decision to divorce him. Certainly she stood to enhance her own significance by marrying the wealthy tetrarch Antipas. When Herodias decided to divorce Herod II and marry his half-brother, therefore, one guesses that she felt she was leaving one of her family's ambitionless members for a far more exciting and richer existence. Why should she not trade her ram, a reticent old black sheep of the family, for a flashy fox? The day would come when a voice crying in the desert would give her the answer.

CHAPTER TWO

The Choice to Run with the Fox

*"That stone wall they are building—
any fox going up on it would break it down!"*

(Neh 4:3)

Herodias' life took a dramatic turn during a visit from Herod Antipas, her husband's half-brother and her own half-uncle. Antipas was staying at the coastal residence of Herodias and Herod II while waiting to sail to Rome. At the time, probably between 21 and 23 C.E., Antipas had been the tetrarch of Galilee and Peraea for more than two decades. Long established in his client role under the Romans, Antipas had built numerous cities and erected various new palaces for himself. When he stopped for a brief time with his brother and sister-in-law Antipas was a powerful, wealthy key player in the political events of his part of the empire. In contrast, his niece Herodias was firmly bound into Herod II's political and economic marginalization. Did it seem to her that while Antipas was on his way to the imperial capital she was going nowhere?

The Pedigree of Antipas

Born around 20 B.C.E., Antipas was one of Herod the Great's three children by his Samaritan wife, Malthace; the other two were a son, Archelaus, and a daughter, Olympias. During Antipas' childhood education one of his companions was Manaen, named in Acts 13:1 as Antipas' *syntrophos,* i.e., foster-brother or intimate friend. As a young man Antipas went to Rome to study and socialize with the imperial family. He was back in Judea no later than 4 B.C.E. during the months preceding his father's death.

19

Malthace's Samaritan identity had always been considered a disadvantage for her sons' political ambitions. However, Herod's execution of their older half-brothers, Aristobulus, Alexander, and Antipater left Archelaus, Antipas, and another half-brother, Philip, as his major heirs. At the dispute over Herod's will before Augustus in Rome in which Antipas and Archelaus were the main contenders, Herodias, then between age eight and twelve, must have been most aware of Antipas. Perhaps this controversial half-uncle, some four to eight years her senior, made a lasting impression upon the young girl. Likewise, the efforts of Herodias' grandmother Salome on behalf of Antipas during the dispute must have left him indebted to her branch of the family.

The Tetrarch's Hunting Grounds and His Nabatean Princess

The settlement of Herod's will named Antipas tetrarch over the territories of Galilee and Peraea. Galilee, the more prosperous region, was separated from Peraea by a few miles of the Decapolis, generally the area of the cities of Scythopolis and Pella. In Galilee Antipas rebuilt the city of Sepphoris, surrounding it with strong walls, causing it to become "the ornament of all Galilee" in the estimation of Josephus (*Ant.* 18.27). Antipas renamed it "Autocratoris" in honor of Augustus, who might be called *autocratōr* in Greek (Latin *imperator*). This served as his capital and residence until he built a new city in Galilee, Tiberias, named for the emperor Tiberius.

Tiberias was founded in about 19 and built on the narrow coastal plain of the west shore of the Sea of Galilee. Because tombs were discovered during the construction of the city, the site was considered unclean by the Jews. This forced Antipas to settle the city with a mixed population of Jews and Gentiles, characterized by Josephus as "a promiscuous rabble" (*Ant.* 18.37). The population of Tiberias may have reached 25,000 under Antipas' rule.[1]

In Peraea, Antipas fortified Betharamphtha, renaming it "Livias" in honor of Livia. Peraea shared a long border with Nabatea, so political motivation may explain why Antipas married a daughter of the Nabatean king, Aretas IV. Three facts support the theory that this marriage was effectively a peace treaty:[2] First, before the marriage there had been great animosity between the Arabs and the Herodians and thus a need to restore

---

[1] Harold W. Hoehner, *Herod Antipas.* MSSNTS 17 (Cambridge: Cambridge University Press, 1972) 52.

[2] Ibid. 130.

peace; second, Josephus comments that Antipas was married to his first wife "for a long time" (*Ant.* 18.109), and in fact Antipas and Aretas got along until after Antipas married Herodias; third, it is known that for the sake of peace Augustus often favored intermarriages among his various client rulers. It is not certain when Antipas married the daughter of Aretas, but these same three points suggest it was in the early years of his tetrarchy and probably before Augustus' death in 14.

The name of this Nabatean princess is unknown, although an inscription has been found at Wadi Musa, a village east of Petra, that lists the members of the family of Aretas IV in the latter period of his reign (9 B.C.E.– 40 C.E.). Of the four daughters of Aretas mentioned, Shaʿudat, Shaqilat II, Gamilat, and Hageru, it has been speculated that Shaʿudat was the wife of Antipas.[3] It appears that Antipas and his Nabatean wife were childless. Given their long marriage, it is doubtful that Antipas suddenly determined to marry Herodias primarily to give him heirs. If Antipas wanted children he would hardly have waited so long or chosen a marriage to Herodias that he knew would unleash politically tumultuous developments.

Preparing to Sail, But the Winds Shifted

"Never dine with another man's wife, or revel with her at wine;
or your heart may turn aside to her,
and in blood you may be plunged into destruction."

(Sir 9:9)

What happened during Antipas' visit to Herodias and Herod II? Josephus describes it this way:

> When starting out for Rome, he [Antipas] lodged with his half-brother Herod, who was born of a different mother, namely, the daughter of Simon the high priest. Falling in love with Herodias, the wife of this half-brother . . . he brazenly broached to her the subject of marriage. She accepted and pledged herself to make the transfer to him as soon as he returned from Rome. It was stipulated that he must oust the daughter of Aretas. The agreement made, he set sail for Rome. (*Ant.* 18.109-11)

Josephus does not say who stipulated that Shaʿudat (assuming that was her name) was to be banished. Herodias is likely to have made the

---

[3] See David F. Graf, "Aretas," *ABD* 1:373–76, at 375.

demand, since Antipas risked serious political problems with the Nabateans by ousting this wife. Yet why did Antipas not insist on keeping his first wife once he married Herodias? Precedent certainly existed, since Herod the Great had maintained multiple wives. In this later period, however, a wife was usually sole mistress of her household.[4] Perhaps Herodias also did not want to live with a Nabatean, whose people were longstanding enemies of the Hasmonean dynasty.[5] Whatever the reason, Antipas agreed to oust his wife, and left for Rome. It is possible that his pact with Herodias was contingent on imperial permission to divorce Aretas' daughter,[6] for by alienating the Nabatean king, whose territory was a buffer between Rome and Parthia, Antipas might cause problems for Rome. The presence and connections of Herodias' mother, Berenice, still living in Rome when Antipas arrived, may have been useful to him in this matter.

A Preference for Arabian (K)Nights

> *"Evil passion destroys those who have it,*
> *and makes them the laughingstock of their enemies."*

> (Sir 6:4)

Sha‘udat somehow got wind of her husband's compact with Herodias and found a way to outwit him. Upon Antipas' return from Rome, and before he knew that she was aware of his intentions to get rid of her, Sha‘udat asked him to send her to Machaerus, a palace/fortress that he controlled near the boundary with her father's territory (*Ant.* 18.111).

> She gave no hint, however, of her real purpose. Herod [Antipas] let her go, since he had no notion that the poor woman saw what was afoot. Some time earlier she herself had dispatched messengers to Machaerus . . . so that when she arrived all preparations for her journey had been made by the governor. She was thus able to start for Arabia as soon as she arrived, being passed from one governor [local sheikh] to the next as they provided transport. (*Ant.* 18.111-12)

---

[4] See Martin Goodman, *The Ruling Class of Judaea. The Origins of the Jewish Revolt against Rome A.D. 66–70* (Cambridge: Cambridge University Press, 1987) 70l; Tal Ilan, *Jewish Women in Greco-Roman Palestine: An Inquiry into Image and Status* (Peabody, Mass.: Hendrickson, 1995) 85–88.

[5] So Hoehner, *Herod Antipas,* 128.

[6] Ibid. 129.

Thus Sha'udat speedily reached her father and informed him of what Antipas planned to do. This precipitated a boundary dispute, or exacerbated one that already existed, between Antipas and Aretas. The tension culminated some years later when Aretas, for the sake of his humiliated daughter, attacked Antipas and defeated him thoroughly.[7]

That Antipas was willing to take on the burden of the enormous problems he would have with Aretas by ousting Sha'udat, as well as the criticism his new marriage provoked in Jewish circles, could be an indication that his liaison with Herodias was, as Josephus states, a love match, at least on his part. Did Antipas also expect to benefit politically by marrying Herodias? It would hardly seem so. By marrying a woman who was a Hasmonean on her mother's side Antipas stood to gain some support from the aristocratic Sadducees, but the tumult he surely could have foreseen from his actions would have argued that he find other ways to achieve political benefits.

She Could Not Divorce, but She Did

In the absence of any details in Josephus about Herodias' divorce from Herod II it is usually assumed that she initiated the process. If she did, such boldness raises the question of her social frame of reference, since Jewish women did not have the prerogative to divorce. In Jewish law divorce was normally seen only as a husband's right and was his to initiate.[8] Roman law, in contrast, allowed a woman to divorce her husband as well as a husband to divorce his wife.[9] Should Herodias' actions therefore be seen as influenced by the Roman affinities of her family?

---

[7] See below, p. 108.

[8] On the debate over whether Jewish women were permitted to divorce see Ilan, *Jewish Women*, 146 n. 31.

[9] On divorce practices among the Romans during this period see Jane F. Gardner, *Women in Roman Law and Society* (London and Sydney: Croom Helm, 1986) 81–95; Susan Treggiari, *Roman Marriage. Iusti Coniuges from the Time of Cicero to the Time of Ulpian* (Oxford: Clarendon, 1991) 435–46. See also Eva Cantarella, *Pandora's Daughters. The Role and Status of Women in Greek and Roman Antiquity* (Baltimore: Johns Hopkins University Press, 1987) 137: "Very rarely in history has there been a conception of such great freedom to divorce, at least at the legal level. Equally remarkable, especially compared with the preceding centuries, is the fact that both men and women had the same rights of divorce." At the same time, as Gardner, *Women in Roman Law* 261, points out: "Whether the incidence of divorce in Roman society was particularly high is not easy to determine. Detailed evidence is lacking to provide anything like a representative sample even of the upper classes."

Since Herodias' grandmother, Salome, decades earlier had ended her marriage to Costobarus, it is evident that at least some women in Jewish circles were able to initiate divorce. Josephus decries this:

> . . . Salome had occasion to quarrel with Costobarus and soon sent him a document dissolving their marriage, which was not in accordance with Jewish law. For it is (only) the man who is permitted by us to do this, and not even a divorced woman may marry again on her own initiative unless her former husband consents. Salome, however, did not choose to follow her country's law but acted on her own authority and repudiated her marriage. . . . (*Ant.* 15.259-60)

Even though Josephus saw Salome as outside Jewish law in initiating her divorce, by sending Costobarus a bill of divorce, a *get* (see Deut 24:1), she was acting partially within Jewish custom. Whether Herodias likewise sent a *get* to Herod II, and whether Herod II gave permission for Herodias' second marriage, Josephus does not say. Nor does he indicate Herod II's attitude toward being abandoned and divorced.

The Herodian women, influenced by the Roman upper class with whom they had cast their lot, probably struggled to claim the privilege of initiating divorce that the relatively more emancipated aristocratic Roman matrons could exercise. Since multiple wives were not permitted in Rome,[10] Roman influence might also have been behind Herodias' demand that Antipas divorce his wife. Furthermore, Antipas, due to his Roman education, may have preferred monogamy himself, although it would cost him dearly in political terms.

An affinity for Roman ways, however, does not mean one should see Herodias, and Salome before her, as operating from more of a Roman than a Jewish frame of reference. Various cultural anthropologists who have studied the kinship customs of the Herodian family observe that as "non-priestly urban elites" the Herodians were thoroughly Jewish in the structure of their kinship but deviated in some ways from what was expected of non-elites. Their status gave them leeway to depart from tradition, to make adaptations that would have accorded with Roman custom and perhaps with the customs of various other non-Jewish groups as well.[11]

---

[10] On Roman marital expectations see Suzanne Dixon, "The Marriage Alliance in the Roman Elite," *Journal of Family History* 10 (1985) 353–78.

[11] See Gerd Theissen, *The Shadow of the Galilean* (Philadelphia: Fortress, 1987) 50–51. Theissen theorizes (202 n. 10) that in obtaining a divorce Herodias was possibly "following not only the Hellenistic and Roman legal tradition but also Aramaic traditions. . . ."

[The Herodians'] status as nonpriestly, urban elites gave them the social flexibility to act in their own (and their family's) interests in terms of honor. While they evidently acted shamelessly in the eyes of Josephus, John the Baptizer and perhaps the general population, the shame of these women [who divorced their husbands] (evaluated positively or negatively) was determined by their own social circles—other (nonpriestly) urban elites—not by Pharisaic interpretation of tradition.[12]

From Josephus data on some eight generations of Herodian marriages has been culled. Analysts have observed that the Herodians practiced a mixture of both endogamy (marriage between close members of a kin group) and exogamy (marriage outside the kin group). Endogamous marriages had the advantage of keeping wealth within a kin group; they also enabled the consolidation of power and protection of the group from outsiders. Both of Herodias' marriages fall into this category. Exogamous unions advanced a family's honor and power by creating links with outsiders, in the case of the Herodians with leaders throughout the eastern Mediterranean. Antipas' marriage to the daughter of Aretas was of this type. This means that when Antipas married Herodias he left an exogamous, political marriage for an endogamous one. It has been suggested that this may have been "an attempt by Antipas to have a more traditional Israelite marriage."[13] Were that true, however, he would hardly have chosen to marry a brother's wife, bringing upon himself the explosive sexual charges that other Jews such as John the Baptist would level against him. Furthermore, Antipas had complicated his life with a double breach of honor toward Herod II: He had intruded on the relationship of a husband and wife, and he had betrayed his brother.[14]

Moving from Brother to Brother: The Date of the Marriage

Josephus offers these details concerning Herodias' transition from Herod II to Antipas:

> . . . Herodias was married to Herod, the son of Herod the Great by Mariamme, daughter of Simon the high priest. They had a daughter

---

[12] K. C. Hanson and Douglas E. Oakman, *Palestine in the Time of Jesus: Social Structures and Social Conflicts* (Minneapolis: Fortress, 1998) 46.

[13] Ibid. 45.

[14] Ibid.

Salome, after whose birth Herodias, taking it into her head to flout the way of our fathers, married Herod [Antipas], her husband's brother by the same father, who was tetrarch of Galilee; to do this she parted from a living husband (*Ant.* 18.135-36).

Josephus bases his charge that Herodias flouted the way of the fathers on two issues: She left one brother by whom she had a child for another brother, and she did so while the first brother was living. We will return to these religious objections to the marriage of Herodias and Antipas, but first let us look at the dating of the event. This text of Josephus might suggest that Herodias married Antipas shortly after the birth of Salome, although it is not certain if he meant "just after" the birth or "some indeterminate time after the fact." Since it is not known when during the marriage of Herodias and Herod II Salome was born, Josephus' information is not helpful in dating Herodias' second marriage.

Assessing that date is problematic. It is related to major questions of first century C.E. Roman and Jewish history as well as the chronology of John the Baptist and Jesus. Among those who have worked on these issues in great detail[15] some scholars have placed the marriage of Herodias and Antipas as late as 35;[16] others have settled on the period between 27 and 31,[17] with yet others judging that it must have been no later than 23.[18] A consideration I find especially germane to dating the marriage concerns events that transpired between Herodias and her brother Agrippa I. An explanation requires recalling the period when Agrippa, Herodias, and their siblings were living with their mother, Berenice, in Rome.

Berenice is known to have asked her friend Antonia to promote Agrippa's prospects. This resulted in Agrippa being raised on familiar terms with Antonia's son Claudius and with the son of Tiberius and Agrippina, Drusus II. Agrippa's connections proved invaluable to him later in life. The cost of pursuing such friendships, however, was very high, leading Agrippa to borrow great sums of money. Josephus says Agrippa was "lavish in giving, but so long as his mother was alive, he kept his natural bent concealed.

---

[15] On the chronological interface between the Gospels and Josephus with respect to the events discussed throughout this study see, e.g., Kirsopp Lake, "The Date of Herod's Marriage with Herodias and the Chronology of the Gospels," *Expositor,* 8th series, 4 (1912) 462–77; Christiane Saulnier, "Hérode Antipas et Jean le Baptiste. Quelques remarques sur les confusions chronologiques de Flavius Josèphe," *Revue Biblique* 91 (1984) 362–76; Nikos Kokkinos, "Which Salome Did Aristobulus Marry?" *Palestine Exploration Quarterly* 118 (1986) 33–50.

[16] Lake, "Date of Herod's Marriage with Herodias," 466.

[17] See Hoehner, *Herod Antipas,* 130–31; Schwartz, *Agrippa I,* 46–47.

[18] Saulnier, "Hérode Antipas," 365–67.

It seemed best not to encounter the burst of temper that anything like that would have provoked in her" (*Ant.* 18.144-45). After Berenice died in Rome in about 23 Agrippa ran into serious debt and was forced, probably in 24, to leave Rome to escape the hounding of his creditors. The death in 23 of his friend, Drusus II, also contributed to his decision to leave the city.

Drusus was married to Livia Julia (Livilla), Antonia's daughter. He was poisoned, and rumor suggested that Livilla had been induced to kill him by her lover, Sejanus, an adviser of Tiberius. Tiberius, distraught at the death of his heir apparent, refused to recognize his dead son's friends, including Agrippa. Agrippa was ostracized in his familiar circles.

Agrippa's departure from Rome must thus be dated in late 23 or early 24. Herodias, who helped him financially after he was back in Judea, was able to do so *because she was already married to Antipas.* Thus the dating of Agrippa's return supports a date before 24 for the marriage of Herodias and Antipas. Settling upon this as a *terminus ad quem* for their marriage, we will temporarily suspend discussion of why others prefer to date the marriage later. We turn now to the details of how Herodias helped Agrippa and follow that with more of his own story.

On Being Her (Ungrateful) Brother's Keeper

After the debt-ridden Agrippa returned to Judea he withdrew to the tower of Malatha in Idumea and contemplated suicide (*Ant.* 18.147-48). His wife, Cypros, wrote to Herodias for help. Herodias persuaded Antipas to assign Agrippa a place to live in his new capital, Tiberias, to give him an allowance, and to appoint him the commissioner of markets there.

Tiberias, with its hot springs a mile away at Hammath, was a popular health resort. Antipas had built a stadium, a forum, baths, and a palace for the new city. When he and Herodias were in residence they lived elegantly. Their palace was on the city's acropolis, Mt. Berenice, a height some 650 feet above the lake, west of the coastal plain where the urban settlement had been constructed. Josephus comments that the palace roof was partly of gold and that it contained representations of animals, presumably statues, even though such were forbidden by Jewish law (*Life* 65-69).[19]

---

[19] Josephus observed the palace firsthand since he was in charge of its destruction during the Jewish War. Among its looted contents he says there were "candelabra of Corinthian make, royal tables, and a large mass of uncoined silver" (*Life* 68). On the archaeology of Tiberias see Yizhar Hirschfeld, "Tiberias: Preview of Coming Attractions," *BAR* 17 (1991) 44–51; Yizhar Hirschfeld, Gideon Foerster, Fanny Vito, "Tiberias," *NEAEHL* 4, 1464–73. A fortress appears to have been built later upon the palace. Nothing on the palace itself has yet been published.

Agrippa's position as market commissioner in this vibrant city was an important one. It entailed oversight of the market, regulation of prices, and inspection of weights and measures. He apparently held the post until the early 30s, but he could not long remain in what to him was a demeaning post under Antipas. Following an occasion when both had been drinking and Antipas had taunted Agrippa for being dependent upon his charity, Agrippa left Tiberias. He went to Syria to live with Flaccus, a Roman friend who was the proconsul of Syria (32–35). This lasted until tension also developed with Flaccus, at which point Agrippa returned south to Ptolemais and prepared to return to Rome.

A Worthy Wife . . . with Fundraising Abilities

*"A wife's charm delights her husband,
and her skill puts flesh on his bones."*

(Sir 26:13)

Agrippa desperately needed funds to maintain himself in Italy. After difficult negotiations, given his disastrous financial history, he finally had a loan and was ready to sail. But Herennius Capito, the procurator of Jamnia, heard about the deal and sent soldiers to extract from Agrippa the massive debt he still owed the imperial treasury in Rome. Agrippa nevertheless escaped by sea at night and went to Alexandria, taking Cypros and their children[20] with him.

Once in Alexandria, Cypros arranged a massive loan from Alexander the alabarch. While Alexander had refused the loan to her husband, "for he did not trust Agrippa's prodigal vein," Josephus states that "he did not deny it to Cypros because he marvelled at her love of her husband and all her other good qualities" (*Ant.* 18.159-60). Cypros promised to repay the money herself. After securing the loan she dispatched her husband to Italy and returned with her children to Judea.

Herennius Capito meanwhile informed the emperor that Agrippa had fled without repaying the treasury. Tiberius, then living on Capri, refused any visits from Agrippa until his debt was paid in full. Undismayed, Agrippa arranged yet another enormous loan from Antonia, paid off the imperial treasury, and thus reinstated himself with Tiberius. Josephus explains that Antonia provided this money "both because she still remembered Berenice his mother—for the two ladies had been deeply attached to each other—and because Agrippa had been brought up with Claudius [her son]" (*Ant.* 18.165).

[20] Agrippa II, Drusus, Berenice, Mariamme, and Drusilla.

But socially Agrippa could not afford to default on a debt to Antonia. He therefore borrowed the huge sum of a million drachmas from a man of Samaritan origin, a freedman of the emperor. After paying off Antonia, Agrippa spent the rest entertaining the emperor's nephew, Gaius. Although "creative financing" ultimately secured Agrippa's future, most notably since Gaius became the next emperor, his vicissitudes in imperial circles had only just begun. Meanwhile, back in Judea, Cypros was left to pay the great debt to Alexander the alabarch. How, or even if, she did this is not known. Since her daughter, Berenice, eventually married Alexander's son, Marcus Julius Alexander, their good relations must have been sustained.

Josephus' statements about Cypros in this financial crisis are amazing. She is one Herodian female he praises. We have already noted his comment on Cypros' "love of her husband and all her other good qualities," which Alexander the alabarch found irresistible (*Ant.* 18.159). This positive picture of Cypros contrasts sharply with Josephus' general portrayal of Herodias. Everything Josephus likes about Cypros functions to help or salvage her husband. In contrast, whatever he reports about Herodias, both in what has already been discussed and in further citations to be made below, shows her as defiant or challenging toward her husband or the traditions of "the fathers." Josephus says almost nothing else about these women in themselves, except occasionally to contextualize them genealogically in the Herodian family. They enter and exit his text almost solely in relation to the men around them.

The explanation of Josephus' treatment of Cypros can hardly be that her demure qualities endeared her to men like Alexander the alabarch, so that he gave her a loan. Did Josephus seriously expect his readers to believe that Alexander lent money to Cypros because of her love of husband and other good qualities? Is Josephus perhaps not being devious in this tale, refusing to say that Cypros was probably independently wealthy and therefore was a better risk as a loan partner for Alexander than her husband? After all, throughout many years as the wife of the debt-ridden Agrippa she, with her children, had survived with a certain amount of honor intact. This suggests that Cypros had some resources, just as Herodias is known to have had her own property. When Cypros returned to Judea after securing the loan it was probably to manage her wealth. Josephus, rather than owning up to her apparent independent wealth, seems to have couched his misogynism in paternalistic phrases about her good qualities.

This story of Agrippa, Cypros, and their finances has taken us into the mid-30s C.E. It is necessary now to turn our attention back to the late 20s and developments in the life of Herodias following her marriage to Antipas in about the year 23.

His Instinct to Strike First

Apart from the few times Josephus condescendingly praises or bla-
tantly blames women, most of the time he ignores them. It would not seem
curious therefore that he reports a significant event of the reign of Antipas
without reference to Herodias and her daughter except that the same story
is detailed in the NT, and there the two women are central characters. The
event is Antipas' execution of John the Baptist.

Josephus tells of the death of John in connection with a rousing defeat
of Antipas' troops by the army of his former father-in-law, Aretas. They
had come to blows over a boundary dispute in Gabalis, which was exacerbated by Aretas' anger at Antipas' treatment of his daughter. This conflict
can be reliably dated to 36.[21] Because Aretas was avenging his daughter,
some argue that the marriage of Antipas and Herodias took place shortly
before, thus about 35. That is not a compelling argument for such a late
marriage date, however. First, Aretas may not have acted in haste, but
rather waited some years for the right opportunity to take his revenge.
Also, such a late date would mean that the death of the Baptist (and sub-
sequently that of Jesus also) would have been in the mid-30s, much later
than scholarship generally judges.

Josephus explains that some Jews saw this defeat of Antipas as an act
of divine retribution for his execution of John. That observation occasions
a flashback by Josephus concerning why and how Antipas had decided to
kill him:

> . . . To some of the Jews the destruction of Herod's army seemed to
> be divine vengeance, and certainly a just vengeance, for his treatment
> of John, surnamed the Baptist. For Herod [Antipas] had put him to
> death, though he was a good man and had exhorted the Jews to lead
> righteous lives, to practise justice towards their fellows and piety to-
> wards God, and so doing to join in baptism. In his view this was a
> necessary preliminary if baptism was to be acceptable to God. They
> must not employ it to gain pardon for whatever sins they committed,
> but as a consecration of the body implying that the soul was already
> thoroughly cleansed by right behaviour. When others too joined the
> crowds about him, because they were aroused to the highest degree by
> his sermons, Herod became alarmed. Eloquence that had so great an
> effect on mankind might lead to some form of sedition, for it looked
> as if they would be guided by John in everything that they did. Herod
> decided therefore that it would be much better to strike first and be rid

---

[21] See below, p. 108.

of him before his work led to an uprising, than to wait for an upheaval, get involved in a difficult situation and see his mistake. Though John, because of Herod's suspicions, was brought in chains to Machaerus . . . and there put to death, yet the verdict of the Jews was that the destruction visited upon Herod's army was a vindication of John, since God saw fit to inflict such a blow on Herod. (*Ant.* 18.116-19)

This information about John's arrest and death at Machaerus[22] constitutes Josephus' sole reference to the Baptist.[23] In the context he created for it in the *Antiquities*[24] this material functions parenthetically. Josephus places it within a narrative where he summarizes the friction between Antipas and Aretas. He tells about John's death merely to explain Antipas' military loss as divinely ordered, and casts the story solely in terms of what Antipas did to John. Josephus tells a plausible tale of the tetrarch's political fear of John as a reason to preempt the Baptist's future work.

---

[22] See Stanislao Loffreda, "Machaerus," *ABD* 4:457–58. Located in Jordan, the fortress of Machaerus is at the end of a ridge between two wadis. Now called Mishnaqa, this isolated mountain rises some 700 meters above sea level. Two fortresses were successively built on the site, which Josephus describes as "intrenched on all sides within ravines of a depth baffling to the eye, not easy to traverse and utterly impossible to bank up" (*JW* 7.166). The mountain forms two saddles to the southeast and northwest sides, making it accessible from the Dead Sea on the west or from the region of Madaba on the east. The first fortress on the site, constructed by Alexander Jannaeus about 90 B.C.E., was destroyed in 57 B.C.E. Herod the Great built the second in 30 B.C.E. Control of Machaerus passed to Antipas following his father's death. From 39 to 44 it was ruled by Agrippa I and then passed directly into Roman administration until it was razed by the Romans in 72.

Because of its proximity to Arabia, Herod had regarded this place as deserving his strongest fortification. He enclosed a large area with ramparts and towers and founded a town there, from which an ascent led up to the ridge itself. On the top, surrounding the crest of the mountain, was a wall with high towers at each corner. Within that enclosure was a palace "with magnificently spacious and beautiful apartments" (*JW* 7.175). Numerous cisterns held an abundant supply of water. One probably served as John's prison. Excavation of the *triclinium* (dining room) of the royal fortress shows it was actually two adjacent but independent rooms, probably one for men and one for women. This correlates with the scene in Mark 6:24-25 where Herodias appears to be in a different room from Antipas and his courtiers during his birthday banquet.

[23] The passages on the Baptist in Slavonic Josephus are medieval insertions. See below, pp. 128–29.

[24] Unlike Josephus' information about Jesus, the *Testimonium Flavianum* (*Ant.* 18.63-64), widely regarded as a later interpolation, there is little doubt as to the genuineness of this passage about the Baptist. A summary of the arguments for its authenticity can be found in Louis H. Feldman, "A Selective Critical Bibliography of Josephus," in Louis Feldman and Gohei Hata, *Josephus, the Bible and History* (Detroit: Wayne State University Press, 1989) 330–448, at 429–30.

No one would miss Herodias and Salome in this narrative or even suspect they might have been behind the scenes were it not for the gospel versions of John's last days. The absence of the mother and daughter in Josephus' rendition raises interesting questions. Did Josephus suppress the story? Was he uninterested in various details that were not germane to the political focus in his narrative? Or was Josephus unaware of the tale of Herodias' and Salome's part in John's death? In contrast, where did the synoptic tradition get its story?

Josephus' words about John were written some two decades after Mark's gospel, and perhaps about five years after Matthew. The material about the death of John in each of these sources causes us also to question whether Josephus knew the oral traditions or Synoptic Gospels of the early Christians. We turn now to examine that early Christian tradition, in which Herodias unquestionably engineered the Baptist's execution. These are texts in which a fox gets outmaneuvered not by a Nabatean king but by a mother hen and her chick.

CHAPTER THREE

The Sound and the Fury.
Part I: His Charge

"The impression made [by John] upon Herod's mind was the deeper because John was known to him as a good man and a just. Our sermons derive force from our character. The solid noble character gives weight to the weakest words. A lofty and pure consistency utters what might, from a literary point of view, be of the most imperfect sort, with an accent that makes it eloquent. The grim ascetic, the stern child of the wilderness, draped in camel's hair and fed on locusts and wild honey—he on whom there rested no spot of shame, of foulness or suspicion—said, 'It is not lawful for thee to have Herodias as thy wife.' Who dares interfere with such things now? No man of my acquaintance. What preacher dares interfere with the family life of his congregation? Not one. Are there not families that would absorb libraries of consolation who would resent the faintest approach toward rebuke? If the preacher sees that you are going to marry the wrong man or the wrong woman, dare he interfere? Only at the expense of his head. The law is the same in all ages. Sympathy at a high price, judgment and rebuke at the price of loss, neglect, persecution, martyrdom. If I were to interfere with your marriages . . . what would be your retort? Imprisonment, decapitation. Not in their physical forms—thank God we have outlived that vulgarity; but where is there a man who dare ask if the weights are just and the balances equal . . . ? No man dare interfere with such things now." [1]

[1] Joseph Parker, *The People's Bible. Discourses Upon Holy Scripture. Vol. XIX: Matthew VI–XVI* (New York: Funk and Wagnalls, 1883) 311–12.

John the Baptist was in excellent company when he castigated the tetrarch, Herod Antipas, and his second wife, Herodias, for their marital situation. Prophets like John had challenged royalty throughout biblical history. Maybe John drew the courage to speak out from his predecessors. But one might expect terrible consequences for chastising the high and mighty. The fate of the prophets, their punishments and deaths would become his. He had to have known that. So where did he get his courage?

John's story, like those of other martyred prophets throughout the ages, has a magnetic quality. Whence the power motivating such a life, one given over fully to the demands of God? A believer never brushes too quickly past the story of a martyr. A martyr's courage in the face of torture and death—Could I be so courageous? wonders the believer. Yet the evangelists, especially Mark and Matthew, tell of John's beheading with a surprising dispassion and noticeable lack of interest in how John went through his final ordeal. They give strikingly more attention to the perpetrators of the death, Herodias, her daughter, and Antipas, than they do to the man who lost his head. Mark, in particular, is very interested in his Herodian characters, prompting some to wonder why he tells so much of *their* story.

This is a bloody, impassioned tale about an avenging wife and mother, her compliant yet manipulative daughter, a fearless prophet, and a debauched tetrarch who feared them all. It is found in whole or part in three places in the Synoptic Gospels: Mark 6:17-29, Matthew 14:3-12, and Luke 3:19-20.[2] At first glance one sees that Matthew and Mark tell generally the same story and Luke gives only a short reference to Herodias and her link with the imprisonment of John.

A comparative study of these texts will proceed here on the assumption of Markan priority, namely that the Gospel of Mark was written first. Matthew and Luke wrote later than Mark, and each incorporated much of Mark's material. This approach requires that the information first be studied in Mark. After that it is analyzed in Matthew and Luke, always with an eye on how these two authors kept, deleted, or changed the Markan text.[3]

---

[2] John 3:24 indicates that John was imprisoned, but this gospel gives no details of his execution.

[3] This is the approach found, for example, in the following commentaries: W. C. Allen, *A Critical and Exegetical Commentary on the Gospel according to S. Matthew.* ICC (3rd ed. Edinburgh: T & T Clark, 1912) 157–60; John P. Meier, *Matthew.* New Testament Message 3 (Wilmington, Del.: Michael Glazier, 1980) 160–61; Benedict Viviano, "Matthew," *NJBC* (Englewood Cliffs, N.J.: Prentice-Hall, 1990) 630–74, at 657; W. D. Davies and Dale C. Allison, *A Critical and Exegetical Commentary on the Gospel according to Saint Matthew VIII–XVIII.* ICC (Edinburgh: T & T Clark, 1991) 463. In contrast see Harold W. Hoehner, *Herod Antipas.* MSSNTS 17 (Cambridge: Cambridge University Press, 1972) 113–17. Hoehner sees in Mark and Matthew two separate traditions of the Baptist's death. I disagree

She's in the Text Only Because He Is

As we compare the three evangelists' contextualization of the story we see that on that level they are more concerned with John the Baptist than Herodias, her daughter, or Antipas.[4] Even their attention to John is secondary to their central interest, Jesus. Methodologically this is important, for while Herodias may be the *prima donna* of this study, for the evangelists she is merely one character, albeit a significant one, in John's story, and he in turn is brought into the narrative to explain Jesus. As minor as she is, however, Herodias functions differently for Matthew, Mark, and Luke; each is unique in his editorial treatment of her.

The Basic Version:
Mark's Creation of a Flashback (Mark 6:17-29)

> ". . . *If there be one of you in this crowded gathering who is pursued by the remembrance of his sin, and cannot free himself from dread of its punishment, he is precisely such a witness as was Herod to the retributive government beneath which the world lies. He may be a deist; it matters not; he wants no external revelation to certify him that there is a God who will take vengeance; the revelation is within him, and he cannot disguise it if he would. He may be an atheist . . . he may tell me that he sees no foot-prints of the Deity, either in the melodies or tempests of nature; it matters not; the foot-prints are in his own soul, the voice rings in his own breast. A being with a conscience is a being with sufficient witness of a God.*"[5]

Mark, having mentioned John's arrest in 1:14 as the point when Jesus began his Galilean ministry, structures 6:17-29 as a flashback. It is inserted into the mission of the twelve apostles (Mark 6:7-13, 30). The flashback is occasioned by Jesus' commissioning of the Twelve and his growing reputation (6:14-16), which raised questions about his identity. Some thought that he was the Baptist brought back to life; others called him Elijah or one of the prophets (6:15).[6] According to Mark, when Antipas heard of the

---

with his argument that "Matthew's account is substantially complete in itself" (117), as will be evident below, p. 66.

[4] While each of the synoptic versions refers to Herodias' husband as Herod, he will continue to be referred to as Antipas throughout this study.

[5] Joseph S. Exell, *The Biblical Illustrator: St. Mark* (New York: Fleming H. Revell Co., 1887) 236.

[6] Mark had suggested parallels between Elijah and John and between Jesus and John at the beginning of his gospel in 1:1-15. On Mark's treatment of John and Jesus in 1:1-15 and

powers at work in Jesus he said "John, whom I beheaded, has been raised" (6:16).[7] In saying that, Antipas probably would not have been expressing belief in a vindicating resurrection by God, but rather a superstitious, guilt-laden fear of John's physical resuscitation from the grave.[8] With this remark by Antipas as his point of departure, Mark then recounts how John's death had happened (6:17-29). At the close of the pericope he returns to his narrative about Jesus and the apostles.

Mark may have intended the inserted flashback to foreshadow a time of failure by the Twelve: John's disciples buried their master, but Jesus' would flee, leaving his burial to one outside the Twelve, Joseph of Arimathea. Mark could also have been suggesting an analogy to his readers: Just as the death of John coincided with the initial apostolic mission, so the death of Jesus would give birth to the Christian proclamation.[9]

Cutting, Pasting, and Changing: Matthew's Placement of the Flashback (Matt 14:3-12)

While Mark doubles back to John's death after the sending forth of the Twelve, Matthew, who had anticipated that mission in ch. 10, places Mark's story of John's martyrdom in a context of foreboding opposition, immediately after the rejection of Jesus at Nazareth (Matt 13:54-58).[10] Like Mark, Matthew uses Antipas' speculation (14:1-2) as the occasion to tell about John's death. Earlier, in 4:12, he had indicated that John had been arrested, and in 11:2-7 he reported that the imprisoned John had sent his disciples to Jesus with questions about his identity.

In Matt 14:3-12 the beheading of the prophet John profiles the death of the ultimate prophet, Jesus. This is evident in Matthew's addition at the end of 14:12: "then they went and told Jesus," i.e., they told him what had

---

his probable reliance on Q therein see Jan Lambrecht, "John the Baptist and Jesus in Mark 1.1-15: Markan Redaction of Q?" *New Testament Studies* 38 (1992) 357–84.

[7] See C.E.B. Cranfield, *The Gospel according to St. Mark. An Introduction and Commentary* (Cambridge: Cambridge University Press, 1963) 207: "Does Herod mean simply that Jesus is John the Baptist all over again? Or does he mean that Jesus is really John *redivivus*? We cannot be sure. It is by no means impossible that a guilty conscience working on a superstitious nature should convince him that John had really returned."

[8] So Walter Wink, *John the Baptist in the Gospel Tradition.* MSSNTS 7 (London: Cambridge University Press, 1968) 10.

[9] So Wilfrid Harrington, *Mark.* New Testament Message 4 (Wilmington, Del.: Michael Glazier, 1979) 83.

[10] On Matthew's casting of John the Baptist in his gospel see John P. Meier, "John the Baptist in Matthew's Gospel," *JBL* 99 (1980) 383–405.

happened to his forerunner. But since John had earlier sent these disciples to Jesus, after John's burial they return to Jesus as *his* disciples.

Cutting but Not Pasting:
Luke's Silence about What Mark Said (Luke 3:19-20)

Luke's redaction of the Markan flashback is akin to Matthew's; Luke, too, relates John as prophet with Jesus as prophet. However, Luke's brief reference to the Baptist within his third chapter reflects that his interest is only in John's *arrest* and thus the cessation of John's preaching. Luke does refer later to John's imprisonment when he reports a dialogue between the incarcerated John and his disciples (7:18), and Luke also mentions John's beheading in a passage in which Antipas expresses responsibility for John's death (9:7-9). But in contrast with Mark and Matthew, Luke implies the tetrarch's *disbelief* that Jesus was John raised from the dead (9:9).[11] Most striking of all is that in 9:7-9 Luke makes no mention of the role of Herodias and her daughter in the beheading.

Luke's only reference to Herodias occurs in a brief passage about John's arrest (3:19-20). He embeds these few verses in a lengthy section in which he relates the baptism and mission of Jesus to recent prophetic history, i.e., the mission and preaching of John (3:1-22).[12] In this context the concise report about Antipas, Herodias, and the arrest of John implies that John's mission ended before Jesus' began.[13] Luke sequentially orders the events: First, John is shut up in prison by Antipas, whom he had reproved because of Herodias (3:19-20). Only after John's imprisonment does Jesus begin his ministry (3:21-22).

A Synoptic View:
Mark 6:17-18//Matthew 14:3-4//Luke 3:19-20

When the evangelists' versions of the arrest and death of the Baptist are compared, striking points of similarity as well as contrasts emerge. A general sequential comparison will now be made in this chapter, surveying

---

[11] I. Howard Marshall, *The Gospel of Luke. A Commentary on the Greek Text.* New International Greek Testament Commentary (Exeter: Paternoster, 1978) 357: "The implication [of Luke in 9:9] is that [in the view of Antipas] John . . . could not rise from the dead, despite what people said, so that the puzzle of Jesus' identity remained unsolved."

[12] So, e.g., Eugene LaVerdiere, *Luke.* New Testament Message 5 (Wilmington, Del.: Michael Glazier, 1980) 45–47.

[13] Luke reports about John's imprisonment *before* mentioning the baptism of Jesus. In contrast with the other Gospels, John is not mentioned in Luke's report of Jesus' baptism.

Mark 6:17-18//Matthew 14:3-4//Luke 3:19-20 and the next, covering Mark 6:19-29//Matthew 14:5-12.[14] The exegetical discussion focuses on the elements of the text regarding Herodias, her daughter, and Antipas. Some comments in this and the next chapter treat the evangelists' redaction, although that discussion is mainly reserved for Chapters Five and Six.

Starting with Mark 6:17, we note that Mark links his flashback to the previous text with the conjunction "for," making the whole story an "extended footnote"[15] that tells what led Antipas to conclude that Jesus was John *redivivus*. Matthew retains the "for" in 14:3, where it likewise introduces his version of the story as the explanation for Herod's thinking. Luke, however, in 3:19 changes the conjunction to the adversative "but," since in his context the arrest of John signals the end of his prophetic work.

Mark's reference to Herod in 6:17 is only his second mention of the ruler. Previously he had referred to him as "King" Herod (6:14), a title he did not need to repeat stylistically in 6:17. Later Mark repeatedly calls him "king" (6:22, 25, 26, 27) and has Herod speak of his territory as his "kingdom" (6:23). Since the ruler in question can only be the *tetrarch* Herod Antipas, Mark's use of "king"/"kingdom" is either incorrect or loose. Maybe it was done in courtesy, or perhaps Mark had only fragmentary knowledge of the Herodian rulers and had confused Antipas with Agrippa I, who held the title of king from 41 to 44. Mark's inaccuracy about the title is not surprising, however. It accords with his general lack of reference to rulers, in contrast with Matthew and Luke who situate their narratives in the larger political context.

In 14:1 Matthew corrects Mark 6:14 by labeling Herod "the tetrarch," a title he has no need to repeat in 14:3. In 14:6-9 he further changes his Markan source by leaving out the reference to the kingdom as well as three of Mark's other four uses of "king." Only in 14:9 does Matthew apparently slip and retain one of Mark's instances of "king." Luke also corrected Mark (6:17), adding "the tetrarch" in 3:19. Luke had earlier in his first chapter referred to "King Herod of Judea" (1:5), i.e., Herod the Great, and then in 3:1 to Herod "the tetrarch" of Galilee, i.e., Antipas, reflecting his accurate knowledge of the two men's titles.

The three parallel texts agree that Herod had John put "in prison." Mark says that Antipas "had sent men who arrested John, bound him, and put him in prison" (6:17), while Matthew states that the ruler "had arrested John, bound him, and put him in prison (14:3)." Matthew, presumably for

---

[14] See Appendix B.

[15] Robert H. Gundry, *Mark: A Commentary on His Apology for the Cross* (Grand Rapids: Eerdmans, 1993) 304.

brevity, shifts the action of the verbs he adopted from Mark to imply that Herod himself did the seizing, binding, and imprisoning. Matthew probably did not intend the reader to think Herod did the dirty work, however, since later in the story he shows others carrying out the ruler's orders (14:10-11). Luke completely omits Mark's "arresting and binding" terminology and concisely states that Herod shut up John in prison (3:20). None of the texts shows interest in where John was arrested or in his place of imprisonment, which Josephus states was Machaerus, nor do the evangelists say in the rest of the story where the birthday banquet, execution, and burial of John took place. Their lack of geographical interest suggests that those details were extraneous to their purposes in telling the story.

While all three synoptics link John's incarceration with his criticism of Antipas for his relationship with Herodias, there are different nuances in causality. Mark and Matthew state that John was imprisoned "on account of Herodias" (*RSV:* "for the sake of Herodias"). How Mark, followed by Matthew, envisioned Herodias as connected with this is, however, not evident until later in their narratives. Mark elaborates on the reason for imprisonment with the words "because Herod had married her" (6:17), although this phrasing is awkwardly repetitive[16] in respect to what precedes and follows it. That is probably why Matthew excised it.

Luke, in contrast, calls the imprisonment of John an evil deed that added to "all the evil things that Herod had done" (3:19-20).[17] Also notably at variance with Mark and Matthew, Luke in 3:19 characterizes Herod as having received a *double reproval* from John, first "because of Herodias" and second "because of all the evil things that Herod had done" (which Luke does not identify). Strikingly, however, the Lukan perspective does not attribute the imprisonment to either facet of John's two-pronged rebuke. While John's charge could hardly have endeared him to Herod, in fact Luke does not stipulate the reason for the imprisonment. Did he perhaps

---

[16] A general characteristic of Mark's writing with which both Matthew and Luke had to deal is Mark's duality. This refers to his tendency to write pleonastically, for example, using redundant or double expressions. See Frans Neirynck, *Duality in Mark. Contributions to the Study of Markan Redaction.* BETL 31 (Rev. ed. Leuven: Leuven University Press, 1988).

[17] Joseph A. Fitzmyer, *The Gospel according to Luke I–IX.* AB 28 (New York: Doubleday, 1981) 476, 478, translates the phrase *pantōn hōn epoiēsen ponerōn* as "all his other misdeeds," thus interpreting Luke as saying that Herod's relationship with Herodias was a "misdeed" as well. However, most commentators do not draw out the sense of "other," but read *pantōn hōn epoiēsen* as "all the evil things." Concerning the use in 3:20 of *epi pasin,* literally "above all" (*NRSV:* "all") see Fitzmyer, *Luke I–IX,* 478 and Marshall, *Luke,* 150, both of whom read the phrase as indicating that here is not merely one more incident in the sequence, but the crowning instance.

think the imprisonment was due to circumstances beyond, or not confined to Herodias, or unrelated to her at all, as in Josephus' report? Is this an indication that Luke had more precise knowledge of the Herodians than did Mark and Matthew, who imply that Herodias was the major factor? Could there also be some reason Luke refused to join Mark in attributing to Herodias a role in which she obviously held much power? Or does Luke want to scale down John at this point in his narrative, and therefore downplays Herodias? Later we will return to such questions concerning Luke's editing.

Mark identifies Herodias as Herod's brother Philip's wife (6:17). Matthew also states this (14:3), while Luke simply says that she was "his brother's wife" (3:19). The term "brother" in these passages refers to a half-brother, since Antipas and Herodias' first husband had the same father but different mothers. Whether Mark and Matthew are correct in naming Herodias' former husband as Philip has been debated. It is likely that Mark, followed by Matthew, confused Herodias' first husband, Herod II, as he is identified by Josephus, with the first husband of her daughter Salome, the tetrarch Philip. This theory rests on the assumption that Josephus' knowledge of Herodian genealogy was extensive, and he was more likely correct on this than Mark was. Furthermore, there are other Herodian-related inaccuracies in Mark. Some scholars, however, theorize that Herodias was married to a second son of Herod the Great and Mariamme II, not Herod II, but one named Philip, even though Mariamme II is not known to have had such a son. Still others argue that Herodias' husband, Herod II, actually must have been called Herod Philip or merely Philip. With respect to the latter position John Meier has wryly commented: "To try to save Mark from a glaring historical error, Christian commentators have traditionally spoken of 'Herod Philip' (salvation by conflation), but such a Herodian poltergeist never existed outside the minds of conservative exegetes."[18]

Luke's refusal to follow Mark in naming Herodias' first husband Philip is noteworthy. He was probably correcting Mark's error, as he did with Mark's title of "king" for Antipas. Luke's omission of the name corresponds with an observation that he generally had a better knowledge of the Herodian family than did the other evangelists.

From Mark 6:17 both Matthew and Luke omit Mark's entire phrase "because Herod had married her." They appear either to have been eliminating Markan redundancy or smoothing out the awkward reasoning this

---

[18] John P. Meier, *A Marginal Jew. Rethinking the Historical Jesus. Vol. II: Mentor, Message and Miracles* (New York: Doubleday, 1994) 172. By "conservative exegetes" Meier means those who go to unreasonable lengths to avoid attributing a mistake to Mark.

phrase creates. Less probable is the explanation that Luke and Matthew were reluctant to describe the union as a marriage. Unlikely also is the theory that Matthew and Luke were refining the historical accuracy of Mark's narrative and placing the arrest, and in Matthew's case the beheading of John, in the period before Antipas' actual marriage to Herodias.

Luke's extremely brief account of John in his third chapter does not continue with details about his death. Later in the gospel, however, Luke's reader is informed of the outcome of the imprisonment when Herod states that he had beheaded John (Luke 9:7-9; see Mark 6:14-16). Still, on the whole the Lukan redaction in comparison with its Markan source is striking in its omission of the role of Herodias and her daughter in the death of the Baptist. If we had only the Lukan account of John's imprisonment (3:19-20) it would be unclear what is really behind those verses other than that Luke wants the reader to know that John was in prison before the ministry of Jesus began. They are intelligible only because we have the longer stories of Mark and Matthew. Why Luke chose to omit the full story is very puzzling.

For All to Hear, or Behind Closed Doors?

Both Mark and Matthew detail John's criticism of Antipas in which John, in an implied direct encounter, decries the illegality of Antipas' marriage to Herodias (Mark 6:18//Matt 14:4). The verb used in both is *elegen,* "had been telling," which is in the imperfect tense. Since this indicates repeated action, the texts envision that John spoke out against the marriage more than once. Likewise, in the Lukan phrasing in 3:19 the passive participle *elenchomenos,* "rebuked," implies that Herod was repeatedly castigated. Would John the Baptist, however, have had access to the ears of Antipas, and perhaps Herodias also? Could he have publicly or even privately challenged them, and if so, when and where? Or was John's condemnation of the marriage and "all the evil things" Herod had done (Luke 3:19) conveyed to the royal pair by others?

It could be argued from Mark 6:17, where Herod *aposteilas,* "had sent,"[19] to have John seized, that Antipas was at some distance from the Baptist and therefore may never have heard John's criticism of his marriage before imprisoning him. This scenario envisions encounters (presumably private?) of the Baptist and Antipas as certainly happening during the conversations Mark suggests in 6:20. In that verse the verb *ēkouen* in the phrase *hēdeōs autou ēkouen,* "he liked to listen to him," is also in the imperfect,

---

[19] Matthew 14:3 omits this term.

implying repeated meetings.[20] If the text is read this way, however, it must be asked why Antipas had originally imprisoned John. Did Antipas fear John as a political threat? If so, this interpretation would harmonize with the reasoning Josephus gives for John's arrest and execution. One could then note a progression in Mark "from Herod's imprisoning John out of political fear to his keeping John safe out of religious fear once he came into direct contact with John."[21] Mark's indication in 6:17 that Antipas had imprisoned John "on account of Herodias" would then be a case of his advancing in time what John said directly to Herod after he was imprisoned. In this understanding of the text "John's private rebuke [would lie] behind his beheading rather than behind his imprisonment."[22]

One can assume, however, that Mark intends the reader to picture John's sharp condemnation of Antipas and Herodias as done in public, perhaps within earshot. Since Mark portrays the Baptist as a prophet he may have viewed John in a classic stance of the Jewish prophets, publicly criticizing royal activity when that conflicted with God's will. Such is the assessment of Raymond Collins.[23] He observes that the notoriety of Antipas' marital situation may likewise have been the context in which Jesus would also have criticized the marriage and stated his own teaching on divorce. Collins observes that Mark's description of the Baptist as directing his condemnation against only the male involved in the scandal, Antipas, "rather than against the machinating Herodias," is explainable due to the Palestinian setting.[24]

In a similar vein but from a social analysis perspective K. C. Hanson and Douglas Oakman think Mark envisioned John as "a threat to the honor of Herod and Herodias, because he was an acknowledged prophet holding their marriage up to public ridicule and shame."[25] In Mark's account these authors see an exposition of "the uneasy relationship between elites and peasants"[26] against which the ruling elites, with their troops and their prisons, could use force to preserve the social hierarchy.

---

[20] Gundry, *Mark*, 305, notes that all the main verbs in vv. 18-20 (except for the direct quotation in 6:18) are in the imperfect tense, which "makes concurrent the actions indicated by them."

[21] Ibid. 319.

[22] Ibid.

[23] Raymond F. Collins, *Divorce in the New Testament*. Good News Studies 38 (Collegeville: The Liturgical Press, 1992) 221–22.

[24] Ibid. 221.

[25] K. C. Hanson and Douglas E. Oakman, *Palestine in the Time of Jesus. Social Structures and Social Conflicts* (Minneapolis: Fortress, 1998) 86.

[26] Ibid.

Whether Mark thought that John's rebuke of Antipas was private or public, Matthew and Luke took it to be public and prior to the imprisonment.[27] In Matt 14:4 the "because" clause, unlike the same in Mark 6:17, makes the encounter between Antipas and John the rationale for the statement in 14:3 that Antipas had imprisoned the prophet "on account of Herodias." Since for him the imprisonment follows upon John's critique, Matthew envisioned a condemnation by John either addressed personally to Antipas or conveyed to him by others. Note that Matthew also omits the latter half of Mark 6:20, Antipas' conversations with John during his imprisonment. Luke likewise implies that the two-pronged reproval John launched against Herod preceded the imprisonment, and thus was public in some sense.

The Words of the Prophet

> *"He became to us a reproof of our thoughts; the very sight of him is a burden to us, because his manner of life is unlike that of others, and his ways are strange. We are considered by him as something base, and he avoids our ways as unclean; he calls the last end of the righteous happy, and boasts that God is his father."*

(Wis 2:14-16)

John's pronouncement to Antipas, *ouk exestin . . . ,* "it is not lawful . . ." (Mark 6:18//Matt 14:4), was a typical formula used in the Pharisees' exposition of Jewish Law. Both Mark and Matthew use the expression numerous times either positively or negatively, normally in reference to a matter of the Law. While Mark completes 6:18 by specifying that it was illegal for Antipas "to have your brother's wife," Matthew expresses what was not lawful simply as "to have her."

Mark's wording of the charge could reflect either his redaction of oral tradition or his own composition. Since four decades had passed between John's critique and Mark's inclusion of it in his gospel, decades that included debate in the nascent Christian communities about Jesus' teachings on divorce, the question arises whether Mark's formulation reflects John's historical critique or a charge put in his mouth but bearing more the teaching of Jesus. An answer to this requires an attempt to assess the historical John.

---

[27] Matthew and Luke envision John speaking out harshly to his listeners. In Luke 3:7 John addresses the crowds as "You brood of vipers!" Matthew 3:7 portrays John as saying the same thing specifically to Pharisees and Sadducees coming for baptism.

Mark's tradition that John lashed out against the tetrarch of Peraea and Galilee for his marriage to Herodias is corroborated by Josephus[28] to the extent that he indicates in *Ant.* 18.135-36[29] that the marriage of Antipas and Herodias was viewed negatively. With this scandal an issue in the territories of Antipas, and with John as a prophetic voice in that region, as Josephus also agrees with the Gospels, John *must* have had something to say about this royal marriage. Therefore, while Josephus does not report John's critique himself, it appears Mark is historically correct in stating John's disapproval. The same assumption holds true for Jesus, who must have been drawn into conversation about controversial events in the locales in which he preached.

Whether Mark's formulation of John's charge against Antipas and Herodias is an accurate quotation of John conveyed to him by oral tradition or whether it is wholly or partially Markan composition, Josephus also corroborates the *substance* of what Mark reports John as saying. The issue for Josephus is that Herodias deviated from Jewish tradition, which he specifies as having to do with *marriage to her husband's brother by the same father,* and as taking place while *her husband was still alive (Ant.* 18.136). This closely parallels Mark 6:18, where John tells Antipas he could not have *his brother's wife.* For both Mark and Josephus the issue was not divorce, not even Herodias' initiation of it, and not the alienation of the affection of each other's spouses and thus the causing of two divorces. Nor was the bone of contention remarriage following divorce, or remarriage to a divorced person, or adultery. While these topics might have been part of public controversy the comparison of the texts argues that for both Josephus and Mark *the* objection concerned marriage between a woman and a man who was her living husband's brother (so Josephus, whose critique is stated only with respect to Herodias), that is, between a man and a woman who was his brother's wife (so Mark, who has John direct his charge against Antipas alone).

What Was the Issue?

Historically John would have criticized Antipas and Herodias for violating the Jewish Law's absolute prohibition of marriage between a man and a woman who was married to his brother, as reflected in these passages:

---

[28] While Josephus' major works, *Jewish War* and *Antiquities,* both postdate Mark's gospel (written about 70), NT scholarship generally judges that Josephus did not know Mark's work. Thus Mark and Josephus function as independent witnesses to oral tradition.

[29] Cited above, pp. 25–26.

You shall not uncover the nakedness of your brother's wife; it is your brother's nakedness (Lev 18:16).

If a man takes his brother's wife, it is impurity; he has uncovered his brother's nakedness; they shall be childless (Lev 20:21).

These laws are found in contexts that list sexual partners who were prohibited because of too close a blood relationship. The lists are often referred to as the "incest taboo." To marry a former sister-in-law was thus considered incest. It plunged one into a state of impurity. While readers today might find this prohibition against marriage to former in-laws difficult to understand, in Leviticus the perception was that in-laws actually became one's blood relations.[30] In other words Herodias, by marriage, had been grafted into the genealogy of her first husband, Herod II.[31] Therefore the marriage between her and his half-brother, Antipas, was equivalent to a brother-and-sister (precisely, a half-brother-and-half-sister) marriage, that is, incestuous.

There *was,* of course, a biological relationship between Herodias and Antipas. She was not only his sister-in-law, but also his niece (he was half-brother to her father, Aristobulus). From the Jewish perspective, however, the uncle-niece relationship was not an impediment to marriage.[32] The issue for Herodias and Antipas was clearly that she had been married to his half-brother.

There was, however, an alternative Levitical prescription, levirate marriage, which may have entered discussions about their marriage:

When brothers reside together, and one of them dies and has no son, the wife of the deceased shall not be married outside the family to a stranger. Her husband's brother shall go in to her, taking her in marriage, and performing the duty of a husband's brother to her, and the

---

[30] See Bruce Malina, *The New Testament World. Insights from Cultural Anthropology* (Rev. ed. Louisville: John Knox Press, 1993) 120–21.

[31] On the roots of this thinking in ancient Israel see Frank Moore Cross, *From Epic to Canon. History and Literature in Ancient Israel* (Baltimore: Johns Hopkins University Press, 1998) 7–11.

[32] See Tal Ilan, *Jewish Women in Greco-Roman Palestine: An Inquiry into Image and Status* (Peabody, Mass.: Hendrickson, 1995) 76–77. She notes that for the Herodians, as for royalty of various other cultures, uncle-niece marriages, as well as the marriages of cousins, served to keep property within a family and to provide socially acceptable partners as well. An exception to the general Jewish acceptance of this type of endogamous marriage were the sectarians at Qumran whose Damascus Document 6:17-18 condemns marriage between uncles and nieces.

firstborn whom she bears shall succeed to the name of the deceased brother, so that his name may not be blotted out of Israel (Deut 25:5-6).

In the case of Antipas and Herodias, however, the levirate marriage requirement did not offer them a loophole. First of all, Herod II was still alive, and second, Herodias had a child by him, Salome, and presumably could have eventually borne him a son.[33] Herodias and Antipas did, nevertheless, have some family precedent that they may have cited in support of themselves. At the same time, the story of these relatives who had also had an incestuous marriage may have haunted them as they entered their own unlawful union.

Antipas' older brother, Archelaus, had previously violated the identical taboo. He divorced his first wife, Mariamme,[34] to marry Glaphyra of Cappadocia, formerly the wife of his half-brother Alexander. Glaphyra had borne Alexander two sons before he was executed in 7 B.C.E. (along with his brother Aristobulus, Herodias' father). She had then been married to Juba, king of Libya, who was presumably still her husband, or at least was still alive, when she agreed to marry Archelaus. The marriage of Glaphyra and Archelaus took place about the time he took possession of his ethnarchy in 4 B.C.E. Josephus describes a dream she had when she was Archelaus' wife:

> She seemed to see Alexander standing before her, and in her joy she embraced him warmly. But he reproached her and said, "Glaphyra, you certainly confirm the saying that women are not to be trusted. For though you were betrothed and married to me as a virgin, and children were born to us, you let yourself forget my love in your desire to marry again [to Juba]. But not content even with this outrage, you had the temerity to take still a third bridegroom to your bed, and in an indecent and shameless manner you again became a member of my family by entering into marriage with Archelaus, your own brother-in-law and my own brother. However, I will not forget my affection for you but will free you of all reproach by making you my own, as you were. . . ." A few days after she had related these things to her women friends she died (*Ant.* 17.351-53; cf. *JW* 2.115-16).

The blatant misogynism of this speech, coming either from Josephus' source or his own editing, is striking. It castigates only Glaphyra, who was

---

[33] Herodias may not have been Herod II's first wife, and he may have had children other than Salome.

[34] She may have been Herodias' sister of the same name.

not even Jewish, for the incestuous marriage between her and Archelaus. Josephus somewhat balances this, however, in an earlier observation that Archelaus had "transgressed ancestral law in marrying Glaphyra" (*Ant.* 17.340). He also demonstrates an ironic inconsistency in this text by allowing Alexander to reprimand Glaphyra even for her second marriage, since both the Jews and the Romans, and certainly the Herodians themselves, overwhelmingly encouraged widows not to remain single.

The story of Archelaus and Glaphyra did not have a happy ending. In 6 C.E. Archelaus was removed from office as ethnarch because of his cruelty. He was banished to Vienne in Gaul (Gallia Narbonensis on the east bank of the Rhone). It is not certain whether Glaphyra died before or during the exile. While Herodias and Antipas might have cited them as predecessors in marriage between a woman and her husband's brother, what neither would have known as they began their own illicit marriage some twenty years later was how similar the last chapters of their lives were to be.

If Herodias and Antipas found any sympathy or tolerance for their controversial union it was most likely among those of their own socio-economic status, within their non-priestly urban elite circles. In that Hellenistically influenced aristocratic company, and given that Roman law would not have viewed marriage between a man and his former sister-in-law as problematic,[35] they probably encountered no charge of incest.

To return to the historical critique of John the Baptist regarding Herodias and Antipas, it is clear that John protested their union as incestuous. Furthermore, his rebuke would have carried overtones from Lev 20:21 that Antipas had not only violated Torah but had thereby been rendered cultically impure. But it is also possible that John opposed divorce in itself, even though Jewish thinking at the time generally allowed both divorce and the remarriage of divorced persons. Like the prophet Malachi who had lashed out: "Do not let anyone be faithless to the wife of his youth. For I hate divorce, says the Lord, the God of Israel" (Mal 2:15-16), John may also have been against it. His would not have been the only voice raised in protest, for Jesus, too, spoke against divorce and remarriage. The Qumran community also opposed divorce (see e.g., 11QT 57:17-19). Nevertheless, Mark's use of the legal phrase *ouk exestin soi echein,* "it is not lawful for you to have" (Mark 6:18//Matt 14:4) argues that the major issue for John was not a sectarian position, such as the prohibiting of all divorce with subsequent

---

[35] On the acceptability in Roman law of a woman marrying her former husband's brother see Jane F. Gardner, *Women in Roman Law and Society* (London and Sydney: Croom Helm, 1986) 35–36. The Romans did disapprove of uncle-niece marriages, but they had long been tolerant of that as a widespread endogamous practice among their Judean clients.

marriage seen as adultery, which Jesus would represent. The issue was rather about violation of the Torah's incest laws. This discussion cannot be concluded, however, without raising the intriguing question of whether Mark himself, in spite of his use of the legal phrase, intended *his readers* to perceive incest as John's real objection.

The Evangelists' Views of John's Objection

It may be suggested that Mark himself did not think that John's critique of Herodias and Antipas was about incest. Mark may rather have condemned each of them for divorce and remarriage to a divorced person. A reason for suspecting this is that Mark, who was writing to a primarily Gentile audience and who often clarifies Judaism for his readers, gives them no parenthetical explanation of John's charge against Herodias and Antipas. Would Mark's Gentile readers, for whom brother-and-sister-in-law marriages were permissible, not have found it difficult to understand the Baptist's condemnation, based on a point of Levitical legislation presumably unknown to them? Yet Mark gives them no help in comprehending that the issue was incest.[36]

Mark's lack of a clarifying explanation[37] might suggest that either he or his oral tradition anachronistically interpreted the Baptist's legal objection not in relation to Leviticus but in light of Jesus' teaching. In Mark 10:11-12 Jesus says: "Whoever divorces his wife and marries another commits adultery against her; and if she divorces her husband and marries another, she commits adultery." According to this statement the illegality in divorce and remarriage is breaking the commandment of the Decalogue concerning adultery. If one analyzes the situation of Antipas and Herodias from this perspective, a violation of the Decalogue was worse than an infraction of the incest laws in Leviticus. If Mark thought that way he would have condemned Herodias and Antipas for having divorced and married each other, thus having committed adultery, when historically the Jewish objections which the Baptist represented were quite different, i.e., concerned with incest.

With respect to Mark 10:11-12, if Mark was quoting verbatim from Jesus, then in v. 12 Jesus referred to divorce initiated by women in a situa-

---

[36] While Mark's Gentile readers might have considered an uncle-niece marriage incestuous, Mark never tells them about that relationship between Herodias and Antipas.

[37] Luke offers his Gentile readers no elucidation either of why the Baptist criticized Herod and Herodias. But neither is Luke especially given to offering clarifications of Jewish matters as Mark does. On Matthew's readers see immediately below.

tion where that was illegal (except for someone like Herodias who managed to do what other Jewish women could not). This observation has inspired the suggestion that Jesus' words in Mark 10:11-12 allude to the case of Herodias. However, any thought of Herodias here on the part of Jesus remains most unlikely in light of a detailed form-critical and redactional study of Mark 10:11-12 by Raymond Collins. Following a linguistic, syntactic and narrative analysis of these verses, Collins judges that Mark rather than Jesus was responsible for 10:12, the latter part of the divorce logion.[38] He determines that Mark probably balanced a traditional saying from oral tradition, one based on a prophetic statement by Jesus (v. 11),[39] with his own redactional parallel (v. 12). Collins logically suspects therefore that the women who could initiate divorce whom Mark had in mind as he composed v. 12 were those in his own Hellenistic milieu.

In contrast with Mark's audience, Matthew and his predominantly Jewish Christian readership would have recognized that the Baptist's criticism of Antipas and Herodias concerned incest. There is no reason to suspect that Matthew understood the charge by John differently. His redaction of the Baptist's words, "It is not lawful for you to have . . ." noticeably changes the direct object, "your brother's wife" in Mark 6:18, to "her." This is best explained as a stylistic shortening of the text since Matthew had already indicated that Herodias was Antipas' brother's wife in the previous verse. While Matthew twice refers to Jesus' teaching on divorce and remarriage, in 19:9 (dependent on Mark 10:11) and in 5:32 (taken from Q), nothing suggests that he read John's charge in that light as one of adultery.

As for Luke, his very tight editing removed Mark's formulaic "it is not lawful for you to have. . . ." Luke collapsed the Baptist's whole charge into a phrase stating that Herod had been rebuked by John because of Herodias, "his brother's wife" (Luke 3:19). Luke is succinct, even too much so, for a reader would never realize from his text that Herod and Herodias were married. What does appear essential for Luke to retain from Mark is that she was his *brother's* wife. Because of this some commentators assume that Luke took the charge to be incest. His predominantly Gentile readers would probably not have understood this any more than

---

[38] Collins, *Divorce*, 65–103, especially 102–103.

[39] On the relation of this pre-Markan version of the saying to the Q-form of Jesus' teaching on divorce, see ibid. 218–19. As for the pre-Markan logion in v. 11, as Mark edits it he may have intended an allusion to Antipas' situation. But since there is uncertainty about the original wording of Jesus' teaching, nothing more can be speculated except to note that talk about the ruler's marital situation could have provided an occasion for Jesus to teach on divorce and remarriage.

Mark's. The absence of any explanation in Luke, however, is not surprising. He seems uninterested in the substance of the issue just as he does not care to include the rest of Mark's story about Herodias and the Baptist. This is an element of Luke's broader lack of interest not only in charges of incest[40] but in the related issues of divorce and remarriage. For example, he only once cites Jesus as teaching on divorce, in a brief statement that scholars find most abruptly integrated into his text (16:18, dependent on Q). He also left out the entire narrative about divorce in Mark 10:2-12. This type of material apparently did not either spark Luke's interest or further his purposes.

First Three, Then Two

This chapter has surveyed Mark 6:17-18//Matt 14:3-4//Luke 3:19-20, parallel passages where the synoptic writers indicate that John the Baptist was imprisoned by Antipas, and that this coincided with John's condemnation of the tetrarch's marriage with his brother's wife. That castigation of Antipas and Herodias did not fall on deaf ears; it resulted, according to Mark, in Herodias holding a grudge against John and determining to kill him. Mark tells the rest of the story in fullest detail, while Matthew edits it concisely. Luke, however, decided to jettison Herodias and her daughter at this point. He mentions neither the grudge, the dance, nor anything about the women's role in John's death. Why Luke decided not to tell what Mark says Herodias and her daughter did will invite some further speculation later on. For now we continue with Mark and Matthew.

---

[40] See Acts 25:13–26:32, where Luke never mentions that Agrippa and Berenice, who were brother and sister, were allegedly an incestuous pair.

CHAPTER FOUR

The Sound and the Fury.
Part II: Her Rage

*"Bad as Herod was, Herodias was infinitely worse. Terrible as it is
to be a great sinner, what is that to being a great tempter? We may,
from the force of temptation, be led wrong ourselves; but calmly,
persistently, and in cold blood to say and do and plan things
destructive to the welfare of others is diabolical."* [1]

The stinging words of John the Baptist condemning Herodias' marriage to Antipas led her to take revenge on the prophet. She wanted his
death, but she would have to work behind the scenes to convince Antipas,
the man who held the power she was wont to wield, to carry out her will.
Herodias' eventual success resulted in the fame she has had within the history of Christianity for the past two millennia. Her accomplice daughter
has shared that limelight, often even eclipsing Herodias. Their story will
now be looked at closely in a continuing comparison of the parallel gospel
texts begun in the previous chapter. Here the focus is on Mark 6:19-29//
Matt 14:5-12. One general observation at the outset is that Mark's lengthy
and vivid narrative in 6:19-29 was collapsed into succinct brevity by
Matthew in 14:5-12. Matthew, however, so abbreviated the story as to
leave some links missing.

---

[1] John H. Burn, *A Homiletical Commentary on the Gospel according to St. Mark*
(London: Funk and Wagnalls, 1896) 215.

The Will to Kill

> *"Where there is an untrustworthy wife, a seal is a good thing;*
> *and where there are many hands, lock things up."*
>
> (Sir 42:6)

In Mark 6:17-18 the evangelist refers all action to Herod, i.e., Herod had John arrested, Herod married Herodias, and John had castigated Herod. In 6:19 Mark shifts the action to Herodias when he states that she had a grudge against John and that she wanted to kill him. After this shift Herodias dominates the action for the rest of Mark's story. She drives the events, with her grudge, rooted in John's castigation of Antipas, empowering her.

Mark indicates that Herodias could not carry out her wish to kill the prophet, giving as the reason that Antipas feared John, a fear that, as Mark explains, came from "knowing that he was a righteous and holy man" (6:20). Herod's fear, therefore, restrained Herodias' intent to kill. Mark, however, leaves unsaid what Herod's qualms were about John. Was he concerned that John might call down God's punishment upon him? Or was his anxiety socio-political, a panic that his subjects might respond more to leadership by a moral person than to that of the corrupt Herodians? Whatever the case, Mark states that an outcome of Herod's apprehension was that he *suneterei auton,* "protected him," the imperfect tense of the verb indicating that the imprisonment lasted awhile. When these last words are read in light of the phrase "on account of Herodias" in v. 17 it is evident that Mark is not saying Herod had imprisoned John to appease Herodias, who really wanted him killed. Rather, Herod was *protecting* him. Herod's only means of keeping a lid on Herodias' hate was to put John in a place where she could not wreak her revenge upon him. This is reflected in the *NAB*'s translation of the same phrase as "[Herod] kept him in custody." Mark also comments in 6:20 that when Herod heard John "he was greatly perplexed; and yet he liked to listen to him." This underscores that the grudge was primarily held by Herodias. Mark leaves the impression that Herod might never have incarcerated John had it not been for his wife.

Matthew in 14:5 collapses Mark's vv. 19-20 (three sentences in the *NRSV*) into one statement. Brevity is nevertheless not the most notable feature of Matthew's redaction. Matthew completely erases from Mark that Herodias held a grudge, that it was she who wanted John killed, and that Herod listened to John gladly. Matthew says rather that Herod himself wanted to put John to death. Further, in 14:5 Matthew shifts the focus of Herod's concern away from John, stating that "he feared the crowd."

Matthew roots that apprehension, not as Mark did in John's being right-eous and holy, but in Herod's awareness that the crowd "regarded him as a prophet."[2] Matthew's latter change relates to John's prophetic role and ac-cords with his general contextualization of this story, which uses John's death as a preview of Jesus' own. With Matthew's explanation that Antipas feared the crowd because they saw John as a prophet we hear overtones of the fate of Israel's earlier prophets, put to death by evil leaders, a point Matthew returns to in 23:29-37.

In comparing Mark 6:19-20 with Matt 14:5 one notes that while Mark's story of what led to John's execution focuses upon a revengeful woman whose husband was safeguarding her prey in prison, Matthew's portrays a male ruler who himself desired to kill his stern critic but feared his own people because they held John to be a prophet. Matthew's Antipas thus turns out to be "less ambiguous and more malevolent"[3] than Mark's. This is consistent with Matthew's apparent desire to recast the story to more strongly bear the theme of rulers killing prophets. But Matthew's almost complete removal of Herodias' pivotal role is thereby very puzzling. Why, when the history of the fate of Israel's prophets at the hand of rulers knew both male and female protagonists, does Matthew so severely reduce Herodias' role? This question will be fully taken up later. First, a survey of the rest of the story.

Carpe Diem!

"Let us lie in wait for the righteous man, because he is inconvenient to us and opposes our actions; he reproaches us for sins against the law, and accuses us of sins against our training."

(Wis 2:12)

Mark's story crescendos in 6:21 when he says "an opportunity came," which could also be rendered "an opportune or suitable day came." The occasion was Herod's birthday,[4] on which he gave a banquet for "his courtiers and officers and for the leaders of Galilee." The opportunity can only refer back to the comment in 6:19 that Herodias could not kill John as

---

[2] See Mark 11:32//Matt 21:26 where Matthew found this idea in Mark.

[3] W. D. Davies and Dale C. Allison, *A Critical and Exegetical Commentary on the Gospel according to Saint Matthew VIII–XVIII.* ICC (Edinburgh: T & T Clark, 1991) 471.

[4] On the abhorrence by the Jews of the celebration of birthdays and whether this was indeed Herod's birthday or the anniversary of his accession see Harold W. Hoehner, *Herod Antipas.* MSSNTS 17 (Cambridge: Cambridge University Press, 1972)160–61.

she wished. Thus the *NAB* rendering in 6:21 is "she had an opportunity one day," indicating that Herodias recognized that *her* chance had come.

Matthew 14:6 again abbreviates Mark. Matthew deletes the idea of an opportunity, and thereby Mark's implication that Herodias had been looking for a way to kill John. Matthew further excises the details that Herod gave a banquet on his birthday, and begins very simply "but when Herod's birthday came. . . ." Matthew also deflates the list of attendees, melting them into "the company" before whom the birthday events unfolded. Such cropping of Mark's text has led to the observation that "all but the essentials have been left out. . . . [Matthew] is not interested in telling a good story but in getting to the theological points with as little distraction as possible."[5] In this way Matthew keeps the focus on Herod and *his* desire to be rid of John.

The location of the birthday feast is not apparent to a gospel reader. Some think that Mark had Galilee in mind, perhaps the palace of Antipas and Herodias in Tiberias, due to the attendance by "the leaders of Galilee" (6:21). Matthew removes even that localization. Both narratives allow one to envision any of the residences that Antipas and Herodias might have frequented, since even those in the tetrarch's territory of Peraea would have hosted visiting delegations from Galilee. The gospels thus do not preclude that the birthday event was at the fortress of Machaerus in Peraea, in accord with the information in Josephus that John was imprisoned and beheaded there. For Mark and Matthew, however, the location was obviously irrelevant.

Enter Salome

> *"Do you have daughters? Be concerned for their chastity,*
> *and do not show yourself too indulgent with them."*
>
> (Sir 7:24)

The feast included a dance by a female whose identity poses problems for us.[6] She is not named by either Mark or Matthew. Mark describes her

---

[5] Davies and Allison, *Matthew,* 472.

[6] There is a difficult text-critical problem in Mark 6:22 regarding the daughter. The variants in the Greek text generally result in two different senses:

(1) Some manuscripts have *thugatros autou Hērōdiados,* literally "his daughter, Herodias," among which there are a number of important witnesses (e.g., א B D L Δ 565 *pc*). These inspire translations indicating that the girl was the daughter of Herod, and named Herodias like her mother. This reading results in historical and contextual difficulties, since

as "his daughter, Herodias" (6:22) implying that she was the daughter of Antipas, although later in vv. 24 and 29 he indicates that she was the daughter of Herodias. Matthew, apparently correcting Mark 6:22, consistently identifies her as the daughter of Herodias (14:6, 8, 11).

From very early in the literature of Christianity[7] this dancing daughter of Herodias was assumed to have been the child of her first marriage, Salome, as her name is given by Josephus. Mark's misinformation in 6:17 that Herodias had been married to Antipas' brother Philip actually supports equating the dancing daughter with Salome since it is known, again from Josephus, that she was Philip's wife. Mark, or his tradition, clearly has a related cluster of persons in the story, but they are not always correctly linked.

Antipas is unlikely to have had a daughter by Herodias who was old enough to perform for the crowd, nor to have had a daughter by his first wife with the same name as his second wife. Adding to this unlikelihood, Mark's narrative goes on to say in vv. 24 and 26 that Herodias was the girl's mother. This reading is nevertheless preferred by numerous translators due to the strength of its external attestation (e.g., N[26], although with a D rating). It was adopted by the *NRSV*.

(2) Rather than *autou,* "his," seen in the phrase above, yet other versions read either *thugatros autēs tēs Hērōdiados* (e.g., A C Θ K *f*[13]) or *thugatros autēs Hērōdiados* (e.g., W), resulting in renderings such as "the daughter of Herodias herself" or just "Herodias' daughter" or, as in the *NAB,* "Herodias' own daughter." Some sources have no possessive pronoun and read *thugatros tēs Hērōdiados* (e.g., *f*[1] *pc*), indicating simply that the girl was "the daughter of Herodias." In supporting this second set of variants as original, reading *thugatros* with either *autēs* or *autēs tēs Hērōdiados,* one notes that Mark's context (see 6:24, 28) indicates that the girl was Herodias' daughter. Furthermore, the reading with *autou* "is out of harmony with the narrative, which does not suggest that the illicit union [of Antipas and Herodias] had been of long duration." The royal pair could hardly have been married long enough for Antipas to have fathered a daughter by Herodias who was at the time old enough to dance for the banquet. Matthew's identification of the girl in 14:6 as *hē thugater tēs Hērōdiados,* "the daughter of Herodias," with no serious variants existing to challenge this as his original text, could also suggest that such was the sense Matthew read in the Markan tradition. This is not certain, however, since Matthew might have read *autou* in the original and realized that Mark needed correcting.

We will proceed on the basis of the *NRSV* text, which follows the first sense and refers to the dancer as *thugatros autou Hērōdiados,* "his daughter, Herodias." This reading is the *lectio difficilior,* the more difficult to explain, and hence the more likely reading to have been "corrected" by successive copyists, thus supplying the second group of readings. If accepting the first sense makes Mark wrong historically about the relationship between Antipas and the girl, be that as it may. Since we have already noted other Markan inaccuracies concerning Herodians in this story it will be assumed that he was also wrong about the dancing daughter's relationship with Antipas. We have no reason to think that Mark is not correct, however, in naming Herodias as the girl's mother in 6:24, 26.

[7] See, e.g., the second-century apologist Justin, *Dialogue with Trypho,* 49.

If Salome is indeed the daughter who danced, then information about her can be pieced together from Josephus. Since most of that data concerns her life after the dance, however, it will be treated in a later chapter. What matters about Salome here in surveying Mark's narrative is to determine her age at the time of Herod's birthday party. That may shed some light on the performance itself.

Dancing for Wolves?

> *"[Dancing] . . . may evince a holy excitement, as when David danced before the ark. His dancing would be the hilarious stepping of a soul full of holy triumph. . . . The dancing of Salome was of another kind. The dancing of the ball-room is a pernicious invention to excite criminal passion. It has often led to the sacrifice of chastity, and to murder afterwards to conceal shame. . . . Christian mothers who send their daughters to the dancing-school should remember the mother of Salome."* [8]

The Markan text in 6:22 and later twice in 6:28, taken over only in the latter instance by Matthew in 14:11, identifies the dancing daughter as a *korasion,* the diminutive of *korē,* "a girl." *Korē* also denotes the pupil of an eye or the "apple" of an eye. *Korasion* should not be translated "little girl," however, since Greek popular speech of this period did not necessarily use diminutives in a diminutive sense. This term could designate a small child, but most often it denotes a young girl at or near marriageable age. Mark had previously used the same word twice in 5:41-42 to refer to the daughter of Jairus, who in 5:41 is said to have been twelve years of age.

The question of Salome's age at the time of the dance relates to the type of performance she gave, about which neither Mark nor Matthew gives any details. Readers are left to make their own assumptions and must do so also concerning Mark's point that "she pleased Herod and his guests" (6:22), an observation Matthew takes over, but with the omission of the guests (14:6).[9] Furthermore, interpreting these elements of the story requires considering also Herod's offer in Mark 6:23 to give Salome "even half my kingdom." An interesting summary of the dilemma commentators face in this cluster of considerations has been made by Janice Capel Anderson:

---

[8] H.D.M. Spence and Joseph Exell, eds., *The Pulpit Commentary: The Gospel according to Matthew* (Chicago: Wilcox and Follett, 1909) 84.

[9] No significance should be attached to Matthew's dropping of the entourage; his redaction of the story tends to focus strongly on Antipas.

How does one understand the girl and her dance? How does one understand Herod and his guests' pleasure? The guests named are all elite males. Do we have a king and guests charmed by the innocent dance of his young daughter, the apple of his eye, or do we have a king and his guests aroused—incestuously in the king's case—and hypnotized by an erotic dance, a young nubile body offering an apple like Eve? Readers have answered the question in both ways.[10]

Dubbing these two approaches the proud parent vs. the erotic scenarios, we note first that most interpreters throughout the centuries have preferred the latter, finding heavy sexual overtones in the story. They have seen the dance as the suggestive performance of a girl around marriageable age and the pleasure of Herod and the guests as sexual arousal, which led Herod to recklessly offer Salome half his kingdom. In contrast, the minority view, the proud parent group, has seen no possibility of the dance being erotic, and Herod's promise, if read literally, as preposterous. How could he be willing to give away half his wealth, and furthermore what was not really his, but belonged to the Romans?

Many scholars actually do not find it improbable that a Herodian princess would have sensually danced before guests or that an aroused Antipas could have made so reckless or impossible a promise. As Harold Hoehner comments, "[Antipas] could easily have diverted her to something else if she had been a mere child."[11] While this position recognizes the shocking nature of the scene in its ancient context, there is hesitation to put anything past the Herodians on moral grounds.

Is an erotic dance thus what Mark, or his oral tradition, and then Matthew in turn envisioned as they integrated this story into their gospels? Most commentators, and certainly a great number of preachers, have supposed so. But there is no way to be certain.[12] In the end, because no details about the daughter's age and her dance are given, both become "mirrors in

---

[10] Janice Capel Anderson, "Feminist Criticism: The Dancing Daughter," in Janice Capel Anderson and Stephen D. Moore, eds., *Mark and Method* (Minneapolis: Fortress, 1992) 103–34, at 121.

[11] Hoehner, *Herod Antipas,* 156.

[12] Davies and Allison, *Matthew* 472, muse: "Could the king really have been pleased by Salome's presumably shameless dance before strangers? Although this is the sort of question that the critical scholar must ask, we do not see that it can be answered. For our sources are silent on the considerations which might lead us to an informed judgement. What sort of dance was performed? Was it lewd or unseemly? And what about Antipas' character? Were his scruples such that he would have been troubled by an indecent spectacle? Or should we hesitate to put anything past a man whose father and example was Herod the Great?"

which Herod, Herodias and interpreters are reflected."[13] So what shall be *our* reflection or projection in this mirror?

Promises, Promises

> *"Just for the sake of them that sat with him*
> *At meat, King Herod kept his sinful oath*
> *And slew the Baptist, though his heart was loth*
> *To crown his record with a crime so grim.*
> *We live in fuller day; his light was dim:*
> *Yet oftentimes we make high heaven wroth*
> *By deeds which stay our souls' eternal growth,*
> *To satisfy some senseless, social whim.*
> *We laugh with flippant scorn at what full well*
> *We know we should adore on bended knees;*
> *We trample our ideals 'neath our feet:*
> *And this for no great cause approved of hell,*
> *Which devils might applaud; but just to please*
> *The whims of them that sit with us at meat."* [14]

The Markan and Matthean accounts throughout the rest of the narrative are noticeably similar with respect to the roles of Herodias and Salome. In both Herodias controls her daughter, and Salome, in turn, is submissive to her mother. The Markan text in vv. 22-25 brims with direct quotations of dialogue between Salome and Herod and between Salome and Herodias. In 6:22 Herod says: "Ask me for whatever you wish, and I will give it." In 6:23 he solemnly swears to Salome: "Whatever you ask me, I will give you, even half of my kingdom." The offer of half his kingdom by a petty prince, who ruled by the grace of Rome and did not have the power to give away his jurisdiction, must have seemed as incongruous to Matthew as it does to later readers. In 14:7 Matthew simply reduces Herod's direct statements to Salome to "he promised on oath to grant her whatever she might ask." In Mark's text Herod's doubly expressed wild promise could indicate that he was drunk; Matthew's truncated version implies a more controlled Herod.

---

[13] Anderson, "Feminist Criticism," 121.

[14] This poem is quoted by Edward Hastings, ed., *The Speaker's Bible: The Gospel according to St. Matthew* (Aberdeen: The Speaker's Bible Office, 1939) 2:210. The source is given as E. T. Fowler, *Love's Argument*, 136, with no further publication information.

Mother's Helper

"DOOMED?
I am Salome.
Must I be
the image of my mother?
Her commitment
to lust
and murder
is her ablest talent.
I detest
her perverse joy
in watching me dance
and watching her husband leering
while trusting his lechery
to achieve the prize
of John the Baptist's
head upon a platter
in my obedience
to her whim
and her polluted purpose.
I dance
but wonder why.
Am I, Salome,
doomed and destined
to be another
Herodias
and not a new
woman in my own
fair right?" [15]

Following Herod's oath Mark indicates in 6:24, using the verb *exelthein,* that Salome "went out" to speak with her mother. This, along with two uses of the verb *eiselthein* in vv. 22 and 25, stating that Salome "came in," or "rushed back," suggests that Mark envisions a "stag party."[16] Matthew,

---

[15] Thomas John Carlisle, *Beginning with Mary. Women of the Gospels in Portrait* (Grand Rapids: Eerdmans, 1986) 39.

[16] Robert H. Gundry, *Mark: A Commentary on His Apology for the Cross* (Grand Rapids: Eerdmans, 1993) 305. See Léonie J. Archer, *Her Price Is Beyond Rubies: The Jewish Woman in Graeco-Roman Palestine.* JSOT.SS 60 (Sheffield: Sheffield Academic Press, 1990) 115. Archer reads Mark 6:21 in light of various other evidence she has compiled from

in contrast, in 14:6, 8 removed the in and out references, implying that the girl and her mother were in the men's company when the girl was "prompted" by her mother (14:8), as if from the crowd of observers at the dance. Later, in 14:11, Matthew does say that the girl, to whom the head had been brought from the prison, took it in turn to her mother; this implies that Herodias was elsewhere. This does not mean that Matthew did not picture Herodias as being at the banquet, for, in his removal of the immediacy from Mark's description of John's execution Matthew could have envisioned that Salome delivered the head to her mother hours later.

Matthew's description in 14:8 of Salome as "prompted" by her mother may be more than a simplification of Mark's wordy "she went out and said to her mother" in 6:24. The Markan text carries a nuance of absolute authority by Herodias over her daughter, whose immediate reaction to Herod's offer of half his kingdom is to consult her mother. Matthew's text is more circumspect about Herodias' control. He places Herodias as an observer at the dance, and her prompting may be read as unsolicited by Salome, a demand occasioned more by the aggressivity of Herodias seizing the chance to get her way with John's life than Salome's need to consult her mother. Matthew may not intend to portray the same absolute power over Salome by Herodias as Mark did, although Matthew clearly has Salome deferring to her mother's wish.

Mother Knows Best

> *"His head is presented to Herodias. She rejoices, exults as though she had escaped from a crime, because she has slain her judge. What say you, holy women? Do you see what you ought to teach, and what also to unteach your daughters?"* [17]

In Mark 6:24 Salome is told to ask for "the head of John the baptizer." In 6:25 she returns "immediately" to Antipas and says, with a slight change in John's title, "I want you to give me at once the head of John the Baptist on a platter." The text allows that the stipulation about serving up the head

---

Greco-Roman Palestine to conclude that females were not present at such banquets. Her study determines that domestic sexual segregation of this type, implying separate quarters for men and women, "applied predominantly to certain sections of the urban community and to the wealthier strata of society."

[17] Ambrose, *Concerning Virgins* 3.6.30-31. For this and numerous other quotations from ancient sources on Mark 6:14-29 see Thomas C. Oden and Christopher A. Hall, eds., *Ancient Christian Commentary on Scripture. Vol II: Mark* (Downers Grove, Ill.: InterVarsity Press, 1998) 82–88.

on a platter (*KJV:* charger) may have been Salome's own idea. Matthew in 14:8, omitting the dialogue between Salome and Herodias, simply indicates that after the prompting by her mother the girl said, "Give me the head of John the Baptist here on a platter." This is the only dialogue in Mark 6:22-29 that Matthew retains as direct discourse. Reworking Mark's sense of haste and immediacy, Matthew in 14:8 changes Salome's demand to be given the head "at once" (Mark 6:25) into the notion that she wanted it delivered "here." Due to the reference to the platter, Matthew perhaps views her as meaning "here and now at this banquet." But in removing urgency from Mark's text he may also have intended Salome's demand to mean "here, later today or very soon while these guests are here."

In 6:26 Herod, who implicitly throughout the Markan narrative is an almost innocent victim of Herodias' determination to kill John, is "deeply grieved" (*NAB:* "deeply distressed"). In contrast Matthew, who up to this point has portrayed a revengeful Herod who wanted to put John to death, in 14:9 simply says he was "grieved" (*NAB:* "distressed"). This seems to be a piece of inconsistent editing on Matthew's part, for Herod had now achieved his goal.

Selective Faithfulness

> *"Herod is an illustration . . . of a conscience fantastically*
> *sensitive, while it is dead to crimes. He has no twinges for his sin*
> *with Herodias, and no effective ones at killing John, but he thinks*
> *it would be wrong to break his oath. The two things often*
> *go together; and many a brigand in Calabria, who would*
> *cut a throat without hesitation, would not miss mass or*
> *rob without a little image of the Virgin in his hat."* [18]

Both Mark in 6:26 and Matthew in 14:9 then indicate that despite Herod's grief he acquiesced to the girl's demand "out of regard for his oaths and for the guests." In Mark the result of the pressure put upon him by the oaths and the scrutiny of the company is phrased in the negative: "he did not want to refuse her" (*NAB:* "he did not wish to break his word to her"). Matthew, however, removes this reminder that Herod was under the power of the dancing girl, and states: "He commanded it [the head on a platter] to be given." As with other instances of Matthew's editing earlier in the narrative, this change makes Herod more authoritative in his scenario than in Mark's.

---

[18] W. Sunderland Lewis and Henry M. Booth, *A Homiletical Commentary on the Gospel according to St. Matthew* (New York: Funk and Wagnalls, 1896) 359.

The Axe Finally Falls

> *"Let us test him with insult and torture,*
> *so that we may find out how gentle he is,*
> *and make trial of his forbearance.*
> *Let us condemn him to a shameful death, for,*
> *according to what he says, he will be protected."*

(Wis 2:19-20)

In the more detailed and vivid Markan narrative the king proceeds "immediately," a term Matthew again removed as he had done in Mark 6:25. Mark says the king sent a "soldier of the guard" (*NAB:* "executioner") to bring John's head. His wording in 6:27-28, using numerous verbs in the masculine singular active voice, can be read as saying that this one soldier received the order, went to the prison, did the beheading, brought the head on a platter, and himself handed it to the girl. Mark may not have intended to suggest a one-man show any more than he probably meant Antipas' statement in 6:16, "I beheaded John," to be taken as direct action by the ruler himself. Matthew seems to have noted the looseness of the language, however, and recasts it using passive verbs, e.g., "his head was brought . . . and given to the girl" (Matt 14:11). Style could explain these changes by Matthew. However, since Mark's ambiguous wording hardly allows one to picture Antipas as flanked by a large body of guards ready to carry out his commands, it seems rather that Matthew again found a way to make him look more authoritative. So in Matthew's story Antipas merely commands and John's head rolls. Presumably the execution was carried out through some chain of command Matthew has no need to mention. Both evangelists agree that the beheading was done "in the prison" (Mark 6:27//Matt 14:10).

The Banquet's Last Course

> *"A girl dances, a mother rages,*
> *there is rash swearing in the midst of the luxurious feast,*
> *and an impious fulfillment of what was sworn."* [19]

The presentation of John's head to the dancing daughter and her delivery of it to her mother completes Salome's role in both Mark and

---

[19] Augustine, *The Harmony of the Gospels* 2.33, in Oden and Hall, *Ancient Christian Commentary: Mark*, 85.

Matthew. Both versions are similar in their non-elaboration on the fate of John's head. Herodias is left holding the dish, and gospel readers are left to wonder what she did with it. As for John's body, Mark in 6:29, followed by Matthew in 14:12, rounds out the story by stating that John's disciples came and took it (including the head?). Both imply that the disciples were at some distance from the prison. Mark says "when his disciples heard about it, they came and took his body, and laid it in a tomb." Matthew edits this to say that "the disciples came and took the body and buried it." He adjusts the Markan ending of the tale by adding that John's disciples then "went and told Jesus." Matthew's addition is critical; in his gospel it underscores that John's death previewed what would happen to Jesus.

Post-Mortem

> *"Remember his fate, for yours is like it;*
> *yesterday it was his, and today it is yours."*
>
> (Sir 38:22)

In this and the previous chapter our survey of the synoptic parallel texts has noted both similarities and differences in how the Markan story of Herodias, Salome, Antipas, and the death of the Baptist was taken over by Matthew and to a lesser degree by Luke. We first considered the differing context each evangelist gave to the material. The story Mark told as a flashback, occasioned by speculation about Jesus' possible identity with the Baptist, functions in his gospel to show that just as Jesus' mission emerged from his forerunner's beheading, so did the Christian mission come forth from Jesus' death. Matthew, who also used the material as a flashback, structured it rather to predict in parallel form Jesus' death like that of the prophet before him. Luke, like Matthew, also drew from Mark to relate John as prophet with Jesus as prophet, although more in a sense of chronological sequence that saw John's preaching ended by his imprisonment just before Jesus' mission began.

For Mark and Matthew the vivid details of the events leading to John's decapitation emphasize the undeniable reality of his death. Those circumstances make Herod's identification of Jesus with John (Mark 6:16; Matt 14:2) all the more astounding. As one commentator on Mark has noted:

What mighty powers must be at work in Jesus [in the perception of Antipas] to push the king into identifying him with a man whose head the king himself had seen delivered on a platter to his own dining room, and then to his wife's dining room, and whose corpse had been interred in a different location![20]

It was also observed that Luke preserved only minimal information from Mark and even that in a much redacted form. Effectively, in omitting the rest of Mark's detailed story of the Baptist's beheading Luke removed Herodias and her dancing daughter from the very traditions concerning Christian origins that he said in 1:3 he intended to pass on in an "orderly account." Matthew, in contrast, retained the whole Markan story, though he heavily redacted it. Matthew, a more concise writer, evidently had other agendas as well. For example, he shifts the responsibility for the death of the Baptist away from Herodias as Mark portrays it and squarely onto Antipas.[21] He also strengthens the authority of Antipas throughout the narrative.

This observation of such intriguing elements of redaction suggests that we should next give more attention to Matthew's and Luke's adaptation of Mark's material. Following that, we will take a close look at their source, Mark's story, and address questions about its origin.

[20] Gundry, *Mark,* 306.

[21] Cf. Marla J. Selvidge, "Violence, Woman, and the Future of the Matthean Community: A Redaction Critical Essay," *Union Seminary Quarterly Review* 39 (1984) 213–23. This author states that Matthew, in editing the Markan story of the murder of the Baptist, "heightens the manipulative role of Herodias" (p. 217), yet she offers no support for that judgment. My exegetical overview in this chapter argues the contrary.

CHAPTER FIVE

Demoted by Matthew and Fired by Luke

As Matthew and Luke independently wrote their gospels each integrated sections of Mark into their narratives. When it came to Mark 6:17-29, the narrative about Herodias strategizing to kill the Baptist, Matthew and Luke used the material differently. Matthew took over the story on the whole, but with significant abbreviating and editing.[1] Luke preserved just a minimum of information from Mark's introduction to the tale and jettisoned the rest. As a result early Christian readers who, unlike us, might know only one of the Synoptic Gospels would learn the story with differing details. Readers of either Mark or Matthew would agree that Herodias and her daughter played significant parts in bringing about John's death. But Mark's readers would know about a powerful Herodias who was the protagonist of the story, while Matthew's would think that she was merely her husband's chance accomplice. People aware of Luke alone would have only minimal information, namely that John had condemned the marriage of Antipas and Herodias; they, however, would learn nothing from Luke about what Herodias and her daughter did to cause John's death.

---

[1] A very few scholars hold that Matthew did not get his story from Mark. For example, Harold W. Hoehner, *Herod Antipas.* MSSNTS 17 (Cambridge: Cambridge University Press, 1972) argues against Matthean dependence on Mark, maintaining that there were two independent traditions concerning the Baptist's death. He holds that the divergences between Mark and Matthew, particularly Matthew's contradiction of the Markan story by saying that it was Antipas who wished to kill John, "may be explained on the supposition that in Matthew's abbreviated account there is a desire to come to the point of the narrative, namely, that it was Antipas who in the end was responsible for John's death" (p. 162). Hoehner's objective with respect to these issues of interdependence, however, seems to be to rescue Matthew from the possibility of having edited his Markan source in a conflicting manner.

The comparison of synoptic passages in our preceding two chapters underscored the extent of Matthew's and Luke's revisions of Mark. It was noted that, in contrast with Mark, in Matthew and even in the two brief verses Luke wrote, the responsibility for the fate of the Baptist is shifted from Herodias to Antipas. The extensive amount of adaptation and elimination of the Markan text by Matthew and Luke suggests that more than placement in a new narrative location was behind their redaction. Why did Matthew and Luke treat the Markan tale as they did? Why their shifting of motives and roles, their omissions and rewording? This chapter considers these questions, looking first at the Matthean and then at the Lukan version.

Matthew the Reductionist

The changes Matthew made in Mark's narrative about Herodias resulted in a less coherent story. Matthew so abbreviated and, in a few places, inconsistently edited the text that "one almost gets the impression that Matthew would gladly have omitted it except for the precious themes of increasing rejection and danger [to Jesus] now made brutally plain by the prophetic death of the Baptist."[2] Matthew's skeletal story is puzzling on two accounts: If, as Matthew says, Herod wanted to kill John, why does Matthew say he was grieved by the turn of events leading to John's decapitation? And, how is one to understand Herodias' attitude toward John in Matthew's version, which, apart from stating that the Baptist criticized her marriage, leaves the reader unprepared for her extreme viciousness? For today's readers who, unlike some early Christians, can compare Mark and Matthew, Matthew's changes in the role of Herodias raise another question: Why is the central role she played in Mark's narration diminished in Matthew's?

While our assumption has been that Matthew worked strictly from Mark as he integrated this story into his gospel, it must be considered whether Matthew had other material that affected his editing of Mark. Daniel Harrington asks if perhaps Matthew "knew a story about John's death like the one incorporated into Josephus' *Antiquities* and tried to join it together with Mark's story."[3] Harrington himself leaves the question open. If Matthew did know such a story this might explain why Matthew shifted the desire to kill John from Herodias to Herod and transferred the object of Herod's fear from John to the people. However, since these changes

---

[2] John P. Meier, *The Vision of Matthew* (New York: Paulist, 1979) 96.
[3] Daniel Harrington, *The Gospel of Matthew.* Sacra Pagina 1 (Collegeville: The Liturgical Press, 1991) 217.

can be explained by Matthew's redactional interests there is no reason to suppose that he revised Mark in the light of other data.

A Puzzling Grief

A first issue concerning Matthew's truncated and adapted version deals with why Herod, who in 14:5 wanted to put John to death, is then "grieved" in 14:9. Given the perfect occasion to rid himself of a personally troublesome prophet, and furthermore being able to blame it on his wife and her daughter, why Herod's sadness or sorrow?

Matthew had earlier in 14:5 altered Mark 6:19-20, where Herod *fears John,* to stress Herod's antipathy toward John but *fear of the people.* Therefore one would expect Matthew to have replaced Mark 6:26, "The king was deeply grieved," with "The king was fearful" in 14:9. Instead Matthew merely removes Mark's "deeply," retains the sense of grief, and thereby creates the reader's dilemma about how Herod could have felt regret. Did Matthew use the idea of grief differently even as he took it over from Mark? Or is this a case of inconsistent editing? Along the lines of the first suggestion, Matthew's grief could be interpreted as fear: "Herod's sorrow in v. 9 is nothing praiseworthy; he is afraid of political consequences."[4] Yet if Matthew intended to convey that Herod was apprehensive it seems likely that he would have explicitly used "fear" again in 14:9 as he had in 14:5.

Another explanation is that Matthew retained the reference to grief because of the parallel he saw between the executions of John and Jesus: ". . . Recall that in Matthew Pilate is Jesus' reluctant executioner, and he finally orders the crucifixion only after pressure is brought to bear upon him; see 27:1-26. So just as Pilate is disinclined to do away with Jesus, so is Herod Antipas disinclined to do away with John."[5] This, however, is not convincing. Matthew indeed establishes Pilate's reluctance to order the death of Jesus, for example by the Barabbas incident and Pilate's handwashing. But this suggests that if he wanted to parallel a reluctant Antipas with a reluctant Pilate he would not, in taking over the Markan text, have shifted the blame for wanting to kill John from Herodias to her husband.

One could also suggest that Herod's grief was that he had made a foolish vow, backing himself into a corner.[6] In the end, however, a slip in

---

[4] So Meier, *Matthew,* 160.

[5] So W. D. Davies and Dale C. Allison, *A Critical and Exegetical Commentary on the Gospel according to Saint Matthew VIII–XVIII.* ICC (Edinburgh: T & T Clark, 1991) 474.

[6] A somewhat similar situation is found in the story of Jephthah and his daughter in Judg 11:29-40. It is unlikely Matthew intended to inject allusions of that text into 14:3-12,

Matthew's editing is most likely what occurred, although it does not explain the omission of "deeply." Nevertheless, that Matthew was inconsistent here is supported by another failure to fix the Markan text: Mark 14:9
is also the only instance where Matthew did not correct Mark's use of
"king" for Antipas, even though he had done so in other places. Two in-
consistencies in the same verse suggest that Matthew was distracted at that
point in his editing.

Matthew's Motives

The most intriguing aspect of Matthew's editing is his treatment of
Herodias. By not telling about her grudge against John, and by saying that
it was Antipas who wanted his death, Matthew hardly prepares his readers
for Herodias' brutal malevolence. Matthew makes Herod the focus of the
action, giving the reader insights into *his* thoughts and feelings (14:5, 9),
but nothing is correspondingly told about Herodias. As Harrington has
noted, "In his work of abbreviation Matthew left out mention of Herodias'
resentment of John's claims and thus decreases the dramatic impact. He
makes Herod Antipas into the main opponent and renders the actions of
Herodias and Salome somewhat mysterious."[7]

Why did Matthew deflate Herodias and shift the desire for John's death
from her to Antipas? Further, why did he so severely reduce Herodias'
prominence, yet retain her significant role in John's death? One explanation
has been that Matthew was aligning Antipas with his father, Herod the Great,
who had sought the death of Jesus as an infant (2:13), and with his brother,
Archelaus, whose rule of Judea caused Joseph to settle in Galilee (2:22). In
this alignment "all form a single rank of opposition [to the prophets]."[8]

Another suggestion is that Matthew had a certain sympathy for upper
class women. Shifting the wish for John's death to Herod effectively exon-
erates Herodias and her daughter.[9] Matthew's portrayal of the wife of Pilate
in 27:19 is cited as support for this theory. But an obvious problem with
this explanation is that Herodias and her daughter are hardly declared

---

however. Jephthah's vow is made to God, while Antipas' is to Herodias' daughter, and
Jepthah must kill someone he loves, his daughter, while Antipas is killing an enemy. Nevertheless, both share the grief of having made a carelessly formulated vow that they felt compelled to fulfill.

[7] Harrington, *Matthew*, 215.

[8] Walter Wink, *John the Baptist in the Gospel Tradition*. MSSNTS 7 (London: Cambridge University Press, 1968) 28.

[9] Kathleen E. Corley, *Private Women, Public Meals. Social Conflict in the Synoptic
Tradition* (Peabody, Mass.: Hendrickson, 1993) 160.

innocent by the Matthean editing. Even in Matthew's truncation Herodias comes off as a perpetrator of evil and Salome as a willing accomplice.

Many have proposed that Matthew wanted to stage Antipas as a second Ahab, to parallel him with the king who wanted to remove Naboth in order to obtain his vineyard (1 Kings 21). This, too, is an unlikely explanation, since Matthew's reduction of Herodias' role actually mutes any suggestion that she was like Ahab's wife, Jezebel—for Jezebel, not Ahab, decided upon the killing of Naboth and orchestrated it in 1 Kings 21:1-15 (even though in 21:19 Elijah accuses Ahab of the crime). Matthew's editing, therefore, weakens any allusion to the Ahab/Jezebel story he may have perceived in Mark's text.

With respect to why Matthew even kept Herodias in the story at all, Elaine Wainwright has proposed an explanation drawn from a gendered reading of his text. She observes that Herodias "is presented as deeply embedded in [Herod's] patriarchal family structure—'his brother Philip's wife'—and as his property—'it is not lawful for you to *have* her' (14:3-4)."[10] Wainwright also notes that Herodias is stylized as a murderess and Salome as a seductress, two typical androcentric depictions of the evil female. She suggests that, nevertheless, "their brief appearance creates for the reader an awareness that the opposition to John and hence to Jesus is inclusive of both women and men even though characterized as predominantly male."[11] In Wainwright's view Matthew wants to minimize, yet not erase Herodias. He reduces Herodias to a patriarchally conventional role, but he retains her because he is concerned to show that both men and women were challenged to accept or, as in the case of Herodias, to reject the kingdom.[12]

Interfering Wives

Matthew's portrayal of Herodias intervening to help her husband brings to mind the other political wife-interventionist tradition he uses. In Matthew 27:19 Pilate's wife sends a message to him during his trial of Jesus stating that, because of a dream she had, Pilate should have nothing to do with "that innocent man." Verse 19 is widely agreed to be an element

---

[10] Elaine M. Wainwright, *Towards a Feminist Critical Reading of the Gospel according to Matthew.* BZNW 60 (Berlin and New York: de Gruyter, 1991) 100.

[11] Ibid.

[12] See also Amy-Jill Levine, "Matthew," in Carol A. Newsom and Sharon H. Ringe, eds., *The Women's Bible Commentary* (Louisville: Westminster John Knox Press, 1992) 252–62, at 253: "While Matthew has not designed a community in which women and men have entirely equal roles, the Gospel recognizes the contributions made to the growth of the church by women as well as by others removed from positions of power."

of Matthew's "special material" because it exhibits his particular vocabulary. The event itself, however, was probably not *created* by Matthew. The structure and function of this dream incident in the gospel differs so much from Matthew's five other dream events (1:20; 2:12, 13, 19-20, 22) as to suggest that in 27:19 he was editing a story that had been passed on to him.[13]

Matthew was presumably aware of the story about Pilate's wife as he was editing Mark's version of the Herodias story. Matthew uses the two political wife-interventionist stories analogously, yet antithetically. Within the context of his concern to show that John the Baptist and Jesus shared the same fate Matthew indicates that each was regarded as a prophet (13:57; 14:5), each was rejected by "this generation" (11:16-19), and each died, *sentenced to do so by a ruler whose wife interfered.*[14] In suggesting a parallel between the two interfering wives[15] Matthew mirrors the tense relations in his own milieu between Judaism and Gentile Christianity, evident throughout his gospel. He underscores by his literary structure and content that it was a Jewish woman who rejected the prophet John while it was a Gentile woman[16] who attempted to save Jesus. Matthew appears to have stylized Mark's story of Herodias to bring it into closer conformity with his story of Pilate's wife.[17]

Why was one woman successful and the other not? Wainwright observes that Matthew effectively contrasts Pilate's wife with the surrounding males, the Jewish leaders, and her husband. While she protests Jesus' innocence "her word alone . . . is unable to change the course of androcentric history. It is as if she had not spoken."[18] But how, then, was Herodias successful by her word alone in affecting androcentric history when she, too, was surrounded by males? Was it precisely because she was not alone,

[13] See Florence Morgan Gillman, "The Wife of Pilate (Matthew 27:19)," *Louvain Studies* 17 (1992) 152–65, at 161–64.

[14] See Wainwright, *Feminist Critical Reading,* 285 and cf. Davies and Allison, *Matthew,* 476, who offer a chart of parallels between John's passion and that of Jesus and, without explanation, ignore both Herodias and the wife of Pilate.

[15] These two wives of officials in the Roman administration of Galilee, Peraea, and Judea probably knew each other. While Matthew says nothing about this, Luke indicates that their husbands, Antipas and Pilate, were enemies who became friends. See Luke 23:12 and below, p. 104.

[16] Pilate's wife was most likely a Gentile. By imperial mandate, provincial officials were not allowed during their course in office to marry a woman of the province, except in the official's native province. The Roman governor Felix, however, acted contrary to this law when he married Herodias' niece Drusilla.

[17] Wainwright, *Feminist Critical Reading,* 286.

[18] Ibid.

but had a female collaborator in Salome, that she could have her way among the men who surrounded her?

Restrained by His Papyrus

Even after having recast Herodias as a mere interventionist rather than as the driving force of the narrative, Matthew portrays her as aggressive. Depending on how he envisioned the banquet scene, he may have pictured her in the crowd watching her daughter dance and shouting out that Salome should ask for the Baptist's head. Matthew likewise describes the wife of Pilate as taking matters into her own hands, but she sends her warning to her husband privately. Matthew does not criticize her attempt to influence her husband's political affairs although, of course, in Matthew's view she acts on the side of righteousness.

It is probable that there were additional dimensions besides a gender perspective influencing Matthew's editing. The wife of Pilate was not unsuccessful in Matthew's text merely because she was a lone woman trying to affect men's affairs, nor did Herodias achieve her goal merely because she allied herself with another female. More to the fore in Matthew's gospel is his overriding theme that each woman's prophet was an innocent person who would die an unjust death. Therefore he had to tell the story of each prophet's death with the only successful intervention being the one that chose evil. Herodias got her way because she was allied with evil.

Matthew's editing of Herodias was probably motivated also by a desire to tame her. Some have observed a tendency on Matthew's part to conventionalize women, perhaps in function of what he or his church expected of the behavior of upper class women.[19] Was Matthew aghast at a political wife, especially a supposedly Jewish one, who was as controlling and aggressive as Herodias? If so, his stylizing of Herodias may betray that a tendency to rein in certain women was operative in Matthew's redaction. A similar phenomenon is apparent in Luke's treatment of Herodian women. It is to Luke's redaction of Mark's tale of Herodias that we now turn.

Luke the Squelcher

Our earlier comparison of Luke 3:19-20 with Mark 6:17-29 showed that Luke drew his two verses mainly from Mark 6:17-18. While in 3:19

---

[19] See Howard Clark Kee, "The Changing Role of Women in the Early Christian World," *Theology Today* 49 (1992) 225–38.

Luke retained one of Mark's references to Herodias, he effectively discarded Mark 6:19-29,[20] telling nothing of how Herodias and her daughter manipulated Antipas into beheading the Baptist. Thus while Matthew severely demoted Herodias in reworking Mark's story, Luke all but expunged her from the "orderly account" (Luke 1:1) of what he deemed significant to pass on about Christian origins, and he *totally* erased her dancing daughter, not to speak of the details surrounding John's execution.[21] What is there to be said about Luke's treatment of this long Markan story?

Some have theorized that Luke recognized a legend when he saw one and discarded the story as far-fetched fiction. This interpretation is often related to scholars' impression that Luke knew more about the Herodians and was more interested in them than the other evangelists. This all leads to the question of *what Luke himself thought or knew about the pericope.* Whether or not the story actually happened as Mark tells it, did Luke leave it out because *he* thought it unhistorical?

Luke's description of Herod in 3:19-20 supports a negative answer. Luke characterizes the ruler using an appositive, the first element of which identifies him as having been rebuked by John because of Herodias. The second element of the appositive is that John's rebuke also castigated Herod for all the evil things he had done. This suggests that *the* bone of contention between Herod and John as Luke saw it was Herodias. Luke did not minimize her as just one of many factors in Herod's dealings with John. Further, in 9:7-9 it is evident that Luke knew John was *beheaded.* Interestingly, Josephus' version of John's death[22] does not say how he was killed. Luke's acceptance of the beheading tradition indicates that he did not dispute a major element of the Herodias story. Were there other reasons therefore, besides doubting the general accuracy of the Markan tale, that could have caused Luke to leave it out? Harold Hoehner suggests five possibilities:

> One reason for Luke's omission of the story may have been that he had already included a great deal about the Baptist, as for example his birth narrative. Secondly, since Luke had concluded the content of

---

[20] A discussion of this omission can be found in Hoehner, *Herod Antipas,* 112–13. This includes reference to the theory that the edition of Mark that Luke relied upon lacked this story. Like Hoehner, I think it more probable that Luke found the story in Mark but chose to excise it. This is supported in 3:19-20, where Luke quotes directly from Mark 6:17-18, and in 9:9, where he indicates that he knew John was beheaded.

[21] Other material from Mark that Luke did not take over includes Luke's "Great Omission," Mark 6:45–8:26.

[22] See above, p. 31.

John's preaching near the beginning of his Gospel culminating in the Baptist's imprisonment (3:19-20), it would be unnatural for him to follow Mark in mentioning it again here. . . . Thirdly, having finished with John in 3:19-20, Luke may not have wanted to mix up the Baptist and Jesus stories. Fourthly, it may be that he thought it less important, *either because it did not appeal to him, or because he thought it unsuitable for his special purpose.* Fifthly, in every case Luke's interest in Herod Antipas was in relationship to Jesus, and since this pericope shows no direct relationship to Jesus this may explain its omission.[23]

While each suggestion is plausible, the fourth suggestion strikes me as probable. *Luke left out the story because Herodias is the story.* His treatment of other Herodian women confirms the validity of this suspicion.

Mastered by His Pen

Besides his one reference to Herodias in 3:19 Luke mentions two other Herodian women, Drusilla (Acts 24:24-26) and Berenice (Acts 25:13–26:32). The two women were sisters and Herodias' nieces, daughters of her brother, Agrippa I.[24] In Josephus' narratives they are politically controversial, especially in marital, divorce, and incest-related matters. Josephus' overall portrayal of Berenice as aggressive is challenged by Luke's sketch of both her and Drusilla in Acts as demure, nonintervening consorts. Luke conveys none of the scandalous or aggressive vibrancy Josephus reports in his few references to Drusilla and in his more extensive information about Berenice. This is consistent with the lack of interest we have observed in Luke regarding both the illicit marriage of Antipas and Herodias and Herodias' role in John's death.

Perhaps Luke was no royal scandalmonger, nor did he care to report sensational details about Herodian marriages and other escapades. This contrasts, however, with most ancient "historians" who, like Josephus, fully exploited (heightened and even created) such data. Maybe this type of material simply did not fit Luke's idealistic, theological, or contextual aims. There is reason to suspect, however, that something else may have contributed to Luke's deliberate stylizing and minimalizing of the Herodian women in Acts.

---

[23] Hoehner, *Herod Antipas,* 112–13. Italics added.

[24] On Drusilla and Berenice see my *Women Who Knew Paul.* Zacchaeus Studies: New Testament Series (Collegeville: The Liturgical Press, 1992) 82–90.

The Ladies of the Church

Recent scholarship has observed that Luke is especially interested in women, noting that his gospel mentions more females than do the others.[25] While this once elicited some feminist enthusiasm for Luke, on closer examination it appears that Luke uses women to send a conventionalizing message to his female readers.[26] Luke's women characters tend to be patriarchally correct. This is notably so with the Herodian women, Berenice and Drusilla. Luke portrays them as fitting the upper class ideal of Greco-Roman women, who were to be seen but not heard.[27] This correlates with the observation that Luke, more than the other evangelists, shows interest in the conversion of upper class women.[28] That is reflected, for example, in Luke 18:2; Acts 17:4, 12, and in the conversion of Damaris in Acts 17:34, who probably was from or moved in upper class Athenian circles.[29]

For Luke, Berenice and Drusilla function as paradigms of Greco-Roman conventionality. In the presence of dominant males, and effectively

[25] See Stevan Davies, "Women in the Third Gospel and the New Testament Apocrypha," in Amy-Jill Levine, ed., *Women Like This. New Perspectives on Women in the Greco-Roman World* (Atlanta: Scholars, 1991) 185–97, at 190: "There is a simple solution to the problem of why Luke's gospel contains more stories about women than the others: Luke was writing for an audience wherein women were more numerous. . . . . The evangelist seeks to capture the attention of the female portion of the audience." This statement is applicable likewise to Luke's writing in Acts. From a perspective of reader response analysis some attempts have been made to characterize the female hearers of Luke's gospel and to assess, in light of their supposed prior religious background, what their response to Luke-Acts would have been. See, e.g., Lilian Portefaix, "Women and Mission in the New Testament: Some Remarks on the Perspective of Audience. A Research Report," *Studia Theologica* 43 (1989) 141–52.

[26] See Mary Rose D'Angelo, "Women in Luke-Acts: A Redactional View," *JBL* 109 (1990) 441–61, at 442. For an overview of this shift in assessing Luke's view of women see Robert J. Karris, "Women and Discipleship in Luke," *CBQ* 56 (1994) 1–20, at 2–5.

[27] See Averil Cameron, "Neither Male Nor Female," *Greece and Rome* 27 (1980) 60–68, at 63: ". . . Women remained marginal in the public life of Rome, at all social levels, even in the late Republic and early Empire when a degree of liberation is usually posited for the upper classes. Even at the highest social level the main method open to them for exercising power or influence was intrigue, usually practised from the bedroom. . . . The major outlet for female activity in the Roman world . . . lay in religion. . . . Clearly Christianity benefited from this pool of available converts just as much as rival creeds, and the speed with which converts were won suggests less a rising status for them in their social world, or a real new role now offered to them, than their own lack of public position, which took them to the mysteries, to Isis, and to Judaism as well as to Christianity."

[28] On Luke and upper class women see, e.g., David W. J. Gill, "Acts and the Urban Elites," in David W. J. Gill and Conrad Gempf, eds., *The Book of Acts in Its Graeco-Roman Setting* (Grand Rapids: Eerdmans, 1994) 105–18, at 114–17.

[29] On Damaris see my *Women Who Knew Paul,* 25–27; Ben Witherington III, "Damaris," *ABD* 2:5.

by male invitation, they each listen to a speech by Paul.[30] Not converted, they are nevertheless portrayed as neutral, even unopposed to Paul.[31] But Luke's upper class female readers, for whom aristocrats like Berenice and Drusilla were role models, could thereby hear two messages: (1) the upper class women in Luke's church who had *converted* to Christianity were actually superior to the infamous, wealthier Herodian women, and (2) at the same time Greco-Roman upper class women, converted or not, were to be seen but not heard . . . except when invited for consultation by dominant males. This constitutes an important message from Luke even though the number of wealthy female converts to Christianity was probably low. Such women, through their ability to act in the socially accepted role of patrons and thus as leaders, were significant figures in their churches.

Leadership from the Salons

To understand Luke it is necessary to read his gospel in light of the system of social relationships between individual patrons and their clients. Halvor Moxnes has succinctly defined that system:

> Patron-client relations are social relationships between individuals based on a strong element of inequality and difference in power. The basic structure of the relationship is an exchange of different and very unequal resources. A patron has social, economic, and political resources that are needed by a client. In return, a client can give expressions of loyalty and honor that are useful for the patron.[32]

Greco-Roman society was imbued with the patronage system, and both women and men functioned as patrons and clients. The most famous of upper class female patrons in that milieu was Livia, the wife of Augustus. Her clients included Herodias' grandparents, Herod the Great and his sister Salome, and through them all of the Herodian family.

---

[30] See my "Berenice at Paul's Witness to the Resurrection (Acts 25–26)," in Reimund Bieringer, Veronica Koperski, and B. Lataire, eds., *Resurrection in the New Testament: Festschrift. Jan Lambrecht.* BETL 165 (Leuven: Peeters, 2002).

[31] In Luke's story Agrippa II seems to consider conversion, but this is highly improbable. Just a few years later (ca. 62) he ordered the death of James the brother of Jesus. On the historical level Agrippa II, Berenice, and Drusilla had to have been aware of their father's negative attitude toward the Jesus movement. Agrippa I had ordered James the son of Zebedee beheaded and had imprisoned Peter.

[32] Halvor Moxnes, "Patron-Client Relations and the New Community in Luke-Acts," in Jerome H. Neyrey, ed., *The Social World of Luke-Acts. Models for Interpretation* (Peabody, Mass.: Hendrickson, 1991) 241–68, at 242.

A survey of Luke-Acts reflects that Luke was conversant with patronage as exercised by women, even those not of the upper class. For example, in Acts both Prisca and Lydia are patrons who hosted and led house churches. However, the way women's patronage actually functioned and how Luke thought it *ought* to be exercised are not easy to distinguish. Since Luke does not write objective history, but rather a highly selective narrative, his view of upper class women's patronage may be more prescriptive than it is descriptive. This speculation is behind the observation made above concerning how demure and noncontroversial Drusilla and Berenice are in Acts compared with what Josephus says about them.

One might conjecture, likewise, that Luke omitted the story of Herodias and Salome among other reasons as an editorial dodge away from telling how aggressive and powerful an aristocratic female might be. Even though Herodias and Salome acted in the cause of evil, and Luke could have told their story to condemn them, by not telling it he avoids mentioning clever, forceful action by females. Such material could implicitly encourage wealthy women to be aggressive in the cause of good. That, however, may not have been desirable to Luke.

Luke's choice to be silent about the manipulative Herodias and Salome is not contradicted by his inclusion of traditions about Prisca and Lydia as leaders of churches. The latter were not aristocrats and had limited material and political means within the overall company of church leadership. While they were leaders, nothing in the NT texts suggests that they had power in the wealthier circles of their cities. For Luke, however, to encourage the patronage of women from higher echelons and thereby promote their leadership may have been unsettling. It would have taken authority out of the hands of the generally lower class men and women who comprised the churches' leadership in Luke's time—and whose social status he most likely shared.

For wealthy Hellenistic women one of the few socially permitted activities was religious inquiry and discussion. Therefore Luke's placement of Drusilla and Berenice at scenes in Acts 24–26 where Paul's ideas were being scrutinized is quite appropriate. But involvement with religious groups was also just a step away from assuming patronage over them. Did Luke fear the patronage of very rich women for gender reasons, sociopolitical reasons, or some combination of these? That suspicion is another in an already extended series of guesses. What is certain is that Luke's pen, whether he consciously intended it or not, kept women in his text like Drusilla and Berenice subdued and subordinate to their consorts. As for their aunt, Herodias, Luke's pen all but crossed her out.

The Triumph of Mark's Herodias

Luke's conventionalizing of the Herodian women, corroborated by his relative lack of interest in and overall omission of Herodias in his gospel, parallels our suspicion that Matthew, too, intentionally recast a headstrong Herodian woman into the role of mere helpmate. Such subduing of women by Matthew and Luke is similar to what is reflected in some other Christian writings, such as the Pastoral epistles. For example, Titus 2:5 admonishes women to be submissive to their husbands "so that the word of God may not be discredited" and 1 Tim 5:14 urges younger widows to remarry "so as to give the adversary no occasion to revile us." This suggests that a patriarchally acceptable social order was perceived as necessary for the success of Christian preaching. Thus conventional women served as apologists for the Christian cause. In a similar way I have proposed that Matthew's and Luke's redactional reduction of women such as Herodias and Berenice, females known to have been flagrantly aggressive, was a way to underscore for upper class Christian women the subservience expected of them.

If it was apparently hard or undesirable for Matthew and Luke to let Herodian women be their determined selves on the pages of their gospel texts, it may have been even more challenging for Antipas to live with them. It would have taken more than Matthew's papyrus and Luke's pen for Antipas to rein in Herodias. Even the severe subjugation of Herodias wrought in ink by Matthew, and Luke's refusal to let his pen tell her story held her down only for a while. Because all three of the Synoptic Gospels were passed on to successive generations, in the conflating minds of Christians Mark's vivid and detailed narrative subsumed Matthew's truncation and Luke's squelching. The better story won out in Christian memories. The Herodias of Mark thus survived two devastating attacks by pen on the battlefield of papyrus. Her Markan roots held her and her daughter fast. But what about his version of the story?

CHAPTER SIX

Writ Large by Mark

Mark gives an unusual amount of space to telling how Herodias set up Antipas to accomplish her desired killing of John the Baptist. No other woman in his gospel receives as much attention. Our preceding discussion of Matthew's and Luke's redactions of Mark has showed how their work reflected their apparent dissatisfaction on some levels with Mark's story. This leads us to take a closer look at Mark's version.

Unlike Luke, who omitted most of the narrative, and Matthew, who shortened it awkwardly and changed characters' motives and responsibilities, Mark told a cohesive tale centered on a female protagonist brimming with determination. She propels the action in his story, finding a way to outmaneuver her husband and destroy her enemy. Mark was evidently not averse to portraying Herodias as a powerful protagonist, while Matthew removed her from that role and Luke chose not to spread the story about Herodias and her daughter in any form. Mark betrays an interest in Herodias and, one might say, a tolerance for letting his readers think about her that the other two synoptic writers obviously did not share. Was Mark fascinated with Herodias? Or was he appalled by her? Why did Mark tell *her* long story when it was *John's martyrdom,* not the details of how it was decided upon, that matters in his gospel?

Whence Mark's Tale?

The literary theory of Markan priority, i.e., that Matthew and Luke used the Markan text, holds that Mark had the basic version of the Herodias story, at least as far as extant sources are known. Where did Mark get his data, his longest story about a woman, and his only pericope that is not in a direct sense about Jesus? Did others tell it to him, or was Mark responsible for it in whole or in part?

Studies of the origin of Mark 6:17-29[1] have generally concluded that the tale did not begin with Mark. This conclusion is based, among other reasons, on the detection of Semitic expressions throughout. The pericope must therefore have entered oral, and perhaps even written, form in Aramaic, which suggests a Palestinian origin. Because Mark knew Greek, but apparently not Aramaic, the translation into Greek must have occurred before he learned the story. Its inclusion of Roman or Hellenistic terms with a military flavor, e.g., *chiliarchoi,* "officers" (6:21) and *spekoulatōr,* "soldier of the guard" (6:27), does not contradict the Palestinian provenance; the terms are evidence rather of the Roman influence behind Antipas' administration.[2] In the absence of other sources to which we can compare Mark's version it is difficult to assess his redaction of pre-Markan material. While some have pointed out the presence of various non-Markan expressions, others have countered with a detailed analysis of the thoroughly Markan characteristics throughout the story. Thus Robert Gundry has commented that we "should not underestimate the extent to which Mark uses his own compositional technique in taking over tradition (whether written or oral)."[3]

Palace Informants

If the story happened as told, how would its details have been learned outside palace circles? Who was the source for inside information such as Herodias' grudge against the Baptist, the oath of Antipas, Herodias' manipulation of her daughter after the dance, and the details of John's death? One theory is that there are at least two persons in NT traditions who might have divulged reliable information about the Baptist's death.[4] The first is Joanna, wife of Chuza, who ministered to Jesus and his disciples (Luke 8:3; 24:10). Her husband was Antipas' financial minister and may have been among "the leaders of Galilee" (Mark 6:21) present at Antipas' banquet. Perhaps Joanna gave a firsthand report of John's death to Peter, who later passed it on to Mark. The second possibility is Manaen, Antipas'

---

[1] See Harold W. Hoehner, *Herod Antipas.* MSSNTS 17 (Cambridge: Cambridge University Press, 1972) 117–22; Roger Aus, *Water into Wine and the Beheading of John the Baptist. Early Jewish-Christian Interpretation of Esther 1 in John 2:1-11 and Mark 6:17-29.* Brown Judaic Studies 150 (Atlanta: Scholars, 1988) 39–74.

[2] So Hoehner, *Herod Antipas,* 120.

[3] Robert H. Gundry, *Mark: A Commentary on His Apology for the Cross* (Grand Rapids: Eerdmans, 1993) 312.

[4] Hoehner, *Herod Antipas,* 120–21, 303–306.

friend from his youth who was later a member of the church in Antioch (Acts 13:1). Maybe Mark received the story firsthand from Manaen when Mark himself was in Antioch, or possibly from Peter, who also visited there. As these speculations suggest, details about inner palace events could have entered early Christian traditions via any informants who had links to the Herodians. A more difficult point to assess about the Herodias episode is whether it actually happened as the tradition passed it to Mark and as he narrates it.

What can be said about the historical veracity of Mark's Herodias story? Some scholars have treated it as *mostly legendary with just a small historical kernel;* others have judged it to be *a balanced mixture of the historical and legendary;* yet others have assumed *it is almost pure history.* The major aspects of the text that are repeatedly discussed as indicative that the tale contains fiction are the dance of Salome, the oath of Antipas, and the noncorrelation in details between Mark and Josephus about John's death. The minor facets of the Markan narrative that have raised doubts about its historicity include Mark's mistitling of Antipas as "king" and the mix-up in names concerning Herodias' first husband. These latter points have already been noted as Markan errors, however, and they shed little light on the story's overall veracity.

She Wouldn't, Would She?

The dance of Salome has been cited as major evidence that the story is fictitious, since some dismiss the possibility that a Herodian princess would have performed an erotic dance before a group of men. To do so would have placed Salome in the role of a courtesan or prostitute, the type of woman who typically provided entertainment at banquets. As noted earlier, however, it is unclear whether this was an erotic dance by a mature girl or a cute dance by a child. Furthermore, if it was a sensual performance the loose moral history of the Herodians would not preclude one of their princesses dancing in public.

He Couldn't, Could He?

Also cited as legally and therefore historically impossible is the promise made by Antipas to the dancing daughter. This tetrarch, who ruled only by the permission of the Romans, could not offer to give away half his kingdom; the Romans determined land distribution to and by such petty princes. Yet one could argue that when he made this implausible gesture Antipas was drunk or speaking in hyperbole to emphasize his largesse toward Salome. Both she and his audience would have understood his offer figuratively. If so, then this element of the story, too, cannot be dismissed as absurd.

Who's Telling the Truth?

The lack of correlation between Josephus' version of John's death[5] and Mark's also challenges the latter's accuracy. The absence of Herodias and the dancing daughter in Josephus and his attribution of all responsibility for the Baptist's execution to Antipas suggest a scenario much different from Mark's. In the judgment of many Josephus sketches the more politically, and therefore historically, probable picture.

Contrary to this negative assessment of the historicity of Mark's tale, however, Louis Feldman has pointed out that it is not necessary to posit a contradiction between Josephus and the gospels concerning the reasons why John was put to death: "The Christians chose to emphasize the moral charges that he brought against the ruler, whereas Josephus stresses the political fears that he aroused in Herod."[6] These texts of Josephus and Mark concerning John may thus be seen as mutually illuminating.[7]

In summary, each of the concerns about Mark 6:17-29 that has raised doubts about its historicity can be met with counterarguments. The result of this back-and-forth debate is thus an impasse, leaving open the possibility that events could have happened as Mark describes them. At the same time, finding nothing conclusive against the historicity still does not mean the story occurred as Mark says. *Allowing for the possibility that things could have happened the way Mark tells them does not mean that in fact*

---

[5] See above, pp. 30–31.

[6] Josephus, *Jewish Antiquities.* Books XVIII–XX. LCL 433, translated by Louis H. Feldman (Cambridge, Mass.: Harvard University Press, 1965) 83, n. e.

[7] In this respect John P. Meier, *A Marginal Jew. Rethinking the Historical Jesus: Vol. II: Mentor, Message and Miracles* (New York: Doubleday, 1994) 62, observes that in Luke's special material on the Baptist in 3:10-14, perhaps coming from Q, Luke divides the questioners who went to the Baptist into the crowds, tax collectors, and soldiers. Meier suggests that Luke's "tax collectors and soldiers" actually may define "the others" in Josephus' notation in *Ant.* 18:118 to the effect that it was when "the others" gathered around John that Antipas began to fear his power and thus killed him. In Meier's view the fact that such important props of Antipas' financial and military power as tax collectors and soldiers had come under John's influence may have been the realpolitik consideration that led to the tetrarch's preemptive strike. Meier conjectures that Antipas did not care if some virtuous elite listened to John, but he did care if his tax collectors and soldiers were taking orders from a different commander.

they did! The oral tradition he learned and may have further redacted could simply have been a realistic tale rooted in only *some* historical data.

The Spinning of a Bloody Good Yarn

Some have suggested that early Christianity fabricated the involvement of Herodias and her daughter in the Baptist's death. They tend to acknowledge as historical only those facts that concur with Josephus' account. This would include that Antipas had ordered John put to death (by a means not specified in Josephus). Generally they would also hold as historical that Antipas' marriage with Herodias was controversial, but would not necessarily assume that John had berated the royal couple or that criticism of the marriage had anything to do with his death. This approach attributes the origin of these latter elements and the rest of Mark's story to a combination of tradition and Mark's own creativity. In other words, for these interpreters the roles of Herodias and her daughter, Antipas' promise to Salome, and the subsequent beheading during a meal are legendary embellishments of the story.

If Herodias and the dancing daughter were brought into the story by oral tradition, or even by Mark himself, what suggested the expansion of the tale that way? Why would Mark or Christians before him insert these aggressive, clever women into John's death events? Furthermore, why lay the blame for the prophet's death so heavily on them, even more than on Antipas? The answer is not difficult to guess. A bare-bones statement about the execution of the Baptist, such as that offered by Josephus, would leave people wondering about the specifics of John's death. It is not surprising that oral tradition would supply interesting details to fill lacunae in the story. Many scholars think that the material about Herodias and Salome and the details about John's beheading are such additions, created to satisfy popular curiosity.

To answer why Herodias and Salome were the specific women drafted to fill in the blanks theories of intertextuality, that is the citation of, reference, or allusion to one text by another, have been suggested. Primary among these has been the assertion that Mark 6:17-29 bears overtones of the biblical stories of Jezebel and Esther. For example, Wilfrid Harrington observes:

> It is noteworthy that the differences between Mark and Josephus center on the theme of the banquet and the role of Herodias and so stem mostly from the parallelism of the Marcan story with the stories of Jezebel and Esther. And there is the matter of an Herodian princess

dancing like a slave-girl. The explanation seems to be that Mark has woven colorful and legendary details into his broadly historical narrative of the fate of John the Baptist.[8]

Shades of Jezebel

"In strength of will and unscrupulous carelessness of human life she [Herodias] is the sister of Jezebel, and curiously like Shakespeare's awful creation, Lady Macbeth; but she adds a strain of sensuous passion to their vices, which heightens the horror. Many a shameless woman would have shrunk from sullying a daughter's childhood by sending her to play the part of a shameless dancing-girl before a crew of half-tipsy revelers, and from teaching her young lips to ask for murder. But Herodias sticks at nothing, and is as insensible to the duty of a mother as to that of a wife. We have a hideous picture of corrupted womanhood. . . . Probably she [Salome] was old enough to be her mother's fellow-conspirator, rather than her tool, and had learned only too well her lessons of impurity and cruelty. She inherited and was taught evil; that was her misfortune. She made it her own; that was her crime." [9]

Since Mark 9:13 identifies the Baptist with the prophet Elijah it has been proposed that for him Antipas and Herodias were reminiscent of Ahab and Jezebel, Elijah's enemies in 1 Kings. When Elijah railed against the actions of the royal household Jezebel was out to kill him, while Ahab wavered.[10] Ahab and Jezebel are portrayed with attitudes of vacillation by one and determination by the other in the seizure of their neighbor Naboth's vineyard, like Antipas and Herodias vis à vis the Baptist. And just as Jezebel orchestrated the death of Naboth (1 Kings 21), so Herodias plotted to get rid of John. Furthermore, while Ahab heard out Elijah's accusations (1 Kings 21:17-29), so Antipas, although perplexed by John, "liked to listen to him" (Mark 6:20); later Jezebel, not her husband Ahab, plots the death of the prophet, as does Herodias, not her husband Antipas. However,

---

[8] Wilfrid Harrington, *Mark*. New Testament Message 4 (Wilmington, Del.: Michael Glazier, 1979) 85.

[9] W. Sunderland Lewis and Henry M. Booth, *A Homiletical Commentary on the Gospel according to St. Matthew* (New York: Funk and Wagnalls, 1896) 359.

[10] On Jezebel see Janet Howe Gaines, *Music in the Old Bones. Jezebel through the Ages* (Carbondale and Edwardsville, Ill.: Southern Illinois University Press, 1999); Gail Corrington Streete, *The Strange Woman. Power and Sex in the Bible* (Louisville: Westminster John Knox, 1997) 63–66.

unlike Herodias, who managed to have John killed, Jezebel was unsuccessful in getting rid of Elijah, although she was blamed for having murdered other prophets (1 Kings 18:4).

These comparisons reveal a few distinct echoes of Jezebel and Ahab in Mark's story of Herodias and Antipas,[11] although it is unlikely the latter tale was modeled on the former. Apart from being aggressive, manipulative, and antipathetic toward a prophet Herodias shares little else of the personification of Jezebel. For example, Jezebel, the daughter of a Phoenician king, was a *foreign* wife who worshiped idols and violated Israel's law in unjust confiscation of her neighbor's land. Furthermore, she got her due in an ignominious death that took place by her being thrown from a wall, trampled under a horse, and left unburied, a meal for the town dogs (2 Kings 9:30-37). In contrast, Mark's Herodias reaps no punishment at all, nor is there any moral lesson about her behavior attached to the story. She is found at its end triumphantly holding John's head and goes on, for all Mark's readers know, to live happily ever after.

Echoes of the Court of Ahasuerus, Vashti, and Esther

The story of Esther has also been cited as a source for various details in Mark 6:17-29.[12] The banquet given by the Persian king Ahasuerus (Xerxes I) for "all his officials and ministers" (Esth 1:13; 2:18) parallels that given by Antipas for "his courtiers and officers and for the leaders of Galilee" (Mark 6:21). Queen Vashti's refusal to obey the king's command to make an entry into the banquet, possibly to display her beauty in the nude (Esth 1:11-12), mirrors in reverse Salome's willingness not only to be present with the men but also to dance. And King Ahasuerus' words to Queen Esther, "'What is your request? It shall be given you, even half my kingdom'" (Esth 5:3), parallel Antipas' offer to the dancing daughter.[13] Further, some of Mark's terminology echoes the Greek (LXX) of Esther. For example, the combination of *korasion,* "girl," with the verb *areskō,* "to please" (Mark 6:22), parallels LXX Esth 2:9 *ēresen autō to korasion,* "the girl pleased him." That Mark inaccurately calls Antipas "king" might also be explained as influence from Esther, where Ahasuerus is frequently so

---

[11] See Streete, *Strange Woman* 150, who observes that because of the ability of Jezebel and Herodias to manipulate and control men "they are tainted by the biblical authors (and subsequent readers) with the reputation for sexual promiscuity, and hence, even though they are clever, are no representatives of Wisdom. Rather, they embody Anti-Wisdom, female sagacity gone terribly 'wrong,' since it is out of male control."

[12] See especially Aus, *Water into Wine,* 39–74.

[13] Cf. Esth 5:6; 7:2; 1 Kings 13:8.

called. But this seems doubtful since Mark, unlike the writer of Esther, does not correspondingly refer to the wife of Antipas as "queen."

In addition to noting links such as these, Roger Aus also sees connections between Mark's tale and the haggadic literature on Esther. He considers the most important rabbinic passages vis à vis the Markan narrative to be *Esther Rabbah* 4/9 on Esth 1:19 and 4/11 on Esth 1:21. These texts concern the manner of Queen Vashti's death. To place the rabbinic comments in context it is necessary to note that Vashti disappears from the biblical story after Esth 1:19, which reports the order that "Vashti is never again to come before King Ahasuerus." Because Esther then replaces her as Queen (2:17), curiosity arose concerning Vashti's fate. The Greek translation (LXX) of Esth 2:1 turns this decree of Vashti's dismissal into a condemnation of her, possibly implying that Vashti was put to death. Various rabbinic sources then used this text as their point of departure for commenting on Vashti's supposed execution.

Aus explains that *Esther Rabbah* 4/9 relates to the offer of Memucan (a minister of Ahasuerus) to send out an order (Esth 1:19). Commenting on this text, *Esther Rabbah* 4/9 adds: "He said to him (the king), 'My lord the king, say but a word and I will bring in her head on a platter.'"[14] Then in a second instance *Esther Rabbah* 4/11 elaborates on the statement in Esth 1:21 that Memucan's advice pleased the king. *Esther Rabbah* 4/11 explains: "He gave the order. And he brought in her head on a platter."[15] Aus notes that, as in Mark 6:27-28, only one person performs the decapitation in the *Esther Rabbah* accounts. While this striking parallelism suggests that John's decapitation and the delivery to Salome of his head on a platter was imported into Mark's story under the influence of rabbinic traditions about Esther, this aspect of Aus's theory is nevertheless improbable because of the uncertainty of the dating of the rabbinic material, which reached final form perhaps as late as 500 C.E., long after Mark's gospel was written in ca. 70 C.E.

As with the possible links between Mark's tale and the Jezebel traditions, a comparison of Mark's narrative with the Esther story again reflects only a few points of similarity. Major differences remain in the characterizations and other elements of the story. Ahasuerus, Vashti, and Esther are not evil characters; furthermore, the point of their story is that Esther used her beauty and risked her life to prevent the destruction of the Jewish people. Apart from Esther's manipulation of the king through her attractiveness, which is mirrored by the effect of Salome's dance, the Esther

---

[14] As cited in Aus, *Water into Wine*, 63–64.
[15] Ibid.

story is a web woven of far different concerns than Mark's tale. He focuses on characters who do evil and whose enemy was a prophet from God. Antipas and Herodias are not concerned to save anyone but themselves. So while it appears that the former story had *some* influence on the latter, *construction* of the latter on the basis of the former is not a sufficient explanation for the genesis of Mark's tale. As C.E.B. Cranfield sums it up: "Perhaps the story of Salome reminded Mark of Esther, with the result that he used some of the language of LXX Esther."[16]

In the end the similarities between the narrative about Herodias and Salome and the stories of Jezebel and Esther are occasional and rather tangential. The few noted elements of intertextuality lead to the conclusion that while it appears Mark 6:17-29 bears minor influence from Jezebel and Esther, an argument that Mark's tale was *formulated* on the basis of either cannot be sustained.

Beheaded by a Woman

". . . I swear that it was my face that seduced him to his destruction."

(Jdt 13:16)

Another biblical *femme fatale* who has been suggested, although less often than Esther and Jezebel, as paving the way for the casting of the female characters, especially Salome, in Mark's story is Judith. A beautiful, wealthy, and respected Israelite widow, Judith set out to save her town of Bethulia during a siege by the Assyrian general Holofernes.[17] Like Esther risking her life for her people, she charmed, tricked, and slew Holofernes, thus demoralizing his army. To do this Judith went into the drunken Holofernes' tent. He had intended to seduce her following a banquet for his personal attendants to which he had also invited Judith. But finding Holofernes lying in a stupor, Judith beheaded him with his own sword. Then she literally bagged his head, putting it in a food sack carried by her maidservant, which they boldly carried out of the encampment.

The parallels with the Markan story are again obvious, particularly the use of sexuality in a banquet context by a woman intent on severing a man's head. Beyond that the similarities between Judith and Salome are not strong. Unlike Judith, Salome is merely her mother's pawn, her demand

---

[16] C.E.B. Cranfield, *The Gospel according to St Mark. An Introduction and Commentary* (Cambridge: Cambridge University Press, 1963) 212.

[17] On Judith see Margarita Stocker, *Judith, Sexual Warrior. Women and Power in Western Culture* (New Haven: Yale University Press, 1998).

for John's head does not seem to have been premeditated, and she and her mother have a goal that is evil in contrast with Judith's. Further, neither Herodias nor Salome actually sliced their victim's head as Judith did (using only two blows! Jdt 13:8). While the Judith story is thus not a strong contender for intertextual influence in a major way upon the Markan narrative, subsequent artistic portrayals of Judith with her bloody trophy in hand and Salome with her weighed-down platter are so similar as to be easily confused.[18] In many representations a sword in the woman's hand is the only sure indicator that the holder of the severed head is Judith.

The possible intertextuality we have so far noted between Mark's story and the traditions of Jezebel, Esther, and Judith represents only one step in mining the subtle allusions that may be borne intentionally or otherwise by the tale of Herodias and Salome. There is also a trove of stories, both biblical and non-biblical, that we can group together as "slayings at dinner." These would have been widely known when Mark's story was formulated and passed on to his generation. To these stories we now turn briefly. Although less frequently brought into discussions of intertextuality than the Jezebel and Esther traditions, they could also have influenced the formulation of Mark's tale.

On the Menu: (Un)Just Desserts

It was not unusual in first-century C.E. Jewish or Greco-Roman lore for someone like Antipas to have killed someone like the Baptist. Stories involving executions at royal dinners may even have influenced the Antipas/John story. For example, in Genesis traditions Joseph, imprisoned with Pharaoh's head butler and baker, tells the baker "'Within three days Pharaoh will lift up your head—from you!—and hang you on a pole; and the birds will eat the flesh from you'" (Gen 40:19). As predicted, "on the third day, which was Pharaoh's birthday, he made a feast for all his servants, and lifted up the head of . . . the chief baker . . . [whom] he hanged, just as Joseph had interpreted to them" (Gen 40:20-21). There is a grim play on words in the original Hebrew, where "lift up your head" is equivalent to being freed from prison. Pharaoh indeed let the baker out of prison, but only in order to have his head.

---

[18] Ironically, while in their biblical contexts Judith is a heroine and Salome a villain, misogynism and ambiguous attitudes about Judith's use of seduction and murder to accomplish her goal have contributed to artistic portrayals that allow her easily to be taken for Salome. Judith is also frequently confused with another heroine, Jael, who killed the sleeping general Sisera by driving a tentpeg through his forehead (Judg 4:17-22). See Stocker, *Judith,* 12–19.

Philo of Alexandria (ca. 20 B.C.E.–ca. 50 C.E.) elaborates on the story in his paraphrastic commentary on this passage. His text, based on the Greek (LXX) version, was generally faithful to the Hebrew, although in Greek the wordplay on lifting up the baker's head is lost. It is consequently missing in Philo. In his text Joseph says to the baker: "The king will order you to be impaled and beheaded, and the birds will feast upon your flesh until you are entirely devoured" (*On Joseph*, 96). Philo's rendition continues:

> . . . When three days had passed, came the king's birthday, when all the inhabitants of the country held festive gatherings, and particularly those of the palace. So, while the dignitaries were banqueting, and the servants were regaling themselves as at a public feast, the king re-membered the eunuchs in prison and bade them brought before him. And, when he saw them, he ratified what had been forecast in the inter-pretation of the dreams, by ordering one [the baker] to be beheaded and impaled and the other [the butler] to be restored to his former office (*On Joseph*, 97–98).

In comparing the Genesis and Philonic versions one notes that while the Genesis text (both Hebrew and LXX) confusingly states that the baker was hanged (40:20), it likewise also says that he was beheaded and im-paled (40:19). The ambiguity disappears if the hanging means that the baker's head was placed on a pole. Philo avoids the confusion by not using the hanging terminology; he sees the event as a beheading and an impaling. Philo also develops the banquet scene beyond the Genesis text, making it clear that the beheading took place during the feasting. In parallel with Mark's story, both Genesis and Philo's paraphrase indicate that the execu-tion was connected with the king's birthday feast. The public flaunting of the baker's head by impaling corresponds also with the presentation to Salome and then Herodias of John's head on a platter.

Yet another banquet-execution incident is recounted by Josephus (*JW* 1.96-98; *Ant.* 13.379-80). He tells that King Alexander Jannaeus in about 90 B.C.E. commanded eight hundred of his captive enemies to be crucified in full view as he feasted with his concubines. So great was the cruelty of this king, one of Herodias' ancestors, that the victims' wives and children were also slaughtered "before the eyes of the still living wretches" (*Ant.* 13.380).

These stories of Pharaoh's baker and Alexander Jannaeus are but two about executions at official dinners that could be cited from Jewish and Greco-Roman literature. Such tales, all very likely embellished in them-selves, could have suggested to Christianity's oral tradition or to Mark himself the idea to situate the Baptist's beheading at a banquet given by

Antipas.[19] But one can also argue that, to the extent that any of these stories has a historical kernel, they may also reflect the reality of brutal power as it was brandished about in ancient court life. Furthermore, Herodias could have drawn inspiration from the same lore, historical or not, to demand a beheading during dinner.

In True Form

Many who have judged Mark 6:17-29 to be non-historical apart from the data it shares with Josephus have held that the genre of the story betrays its fictional nature. Joachim Gnilka has suggested that underlying this pericope is a short tradition along the lines of Jewish martyrology (comprising 6:17-18 and perhaps 6:29), which was then infused with the popular motif of a vengeful woman.[20] Aus argues against this combination, however, noting a Semitic wordplay in vv. 17, 19, and 20 that makes it unlikely that vv. 19-29 were originally separate from vv. 17-18. Aus fully surveys the other genres that have been suggested for Mark 6:17-29, noting that the tale has been classified, for example, as a legend, a popular folktale, and a midrash. He himself proposes that it is an etiological haggada, since "the story not only explains the cause of John's being beheaded . . . but also fills in the manner of the beheading, something typical of haggada."[21]

It may be noted, however, that as a flashback about the Baptist's death Mark's story is surprisingly not too interested in John. No mention is made of his last moments or any final words he may have uttered before the beheading, nor is there any attention given to the fate of his head. John "is not portrayed as a martyr. Nothing is said of his courage in the face of suffering or his unswerving faith in the final triumph of his cause. In fact he scarcely manages to appear in his own death-scene at all! The emphasis is rather on what they do to him."[22]

A further problem with these literary theories, which imply that Mark's story is fictional except when it agrees with Josephus, is the absence of the moralizing tone normally found in most of the proposed genres. Mark sug-

---

[19] The same is true for popularly known stories containing the theme of a ruler being regretfully forced to grant a favor because of inviting someone to make a wish known in public. For examples see Joel Marcus, *Mark 1–8*. AB 27 (New York: Doubleday, 2000) 402.

[20] Joachim Gnilka, *Das Evangelium nach Markus. 1 Teilband: Mk 1–8,26*. Evangelisch-Katholischer Kommentar zum Neuen Testament II/1 (Neukirchen-Vluyn: Neukirchener Verlag, 1978) 245–47.

[21] Aus, *Water into Wine*, 68.

[22] Walter Wink, *John the Baptist in the Gospel Tradition*. MSSNTS 7 (London: Cambridge University Press, 1968) 13.

gests no explicit lesson to the readers. Herodias experiences no retribution for her actions, nor does Salome. Matthew apparently reacted to this, for to the ending of Mark's story he added in 14:12 that the disciples "went and told Jesus." This created a subtle foreshadowing of what would happen to Jesus. While Matthew thus shaped Mark's story to convey a lesson, for Mark it appears to have functioned informatively. In this respect Gundry comments: "The lack of a moralistic tone in Mark [6:17-29] favors history over legend."[23] Harold Hoehner has similarly argued: "There is no good reason for thinking that the story was a legend created out of a religious imagination and fantasy. . . . There is no good reason, therefore, for not believing that the story is true."[24] Are we inclined to agree with these statements?

So far in our discussion of the historicity of Mark's story nothing has convincingly demonstrated that what Mark tells about Herodias and her daughter never happened. For each argument scholars have cited to show that the tale is impossible historically, other have offered counterarguments. While elements of intertextual influence certainly seem present, they are insufficient to explain the construction of Mark's story. Attempts to assign a fictional genre to the pericope have likewise not been convincing. We are thus left with no conclusive proof that the story is fictional apart from aspects of it that agree with Josephus. This leaves open the possibility of its general historicity. Is the story realistic because it is indeed a narrative of actual events? Is there something that can persuade us it is probable?

The School of Salome

The most compelling consideration that allows for the historicity of Mark 6:17-29, in my opinion, is that its description of the actions of Herodias and Salome corresponds with how other Herodian and Roman women around them are reported to have exercised power. This statement must be immediately qualified, however, by reminding ourselves that ancient historiography is permeated with misogynism and often gives scathing caricatures of royal women.[25] How, therefore, can one assess the extent to which hate-filled literary portrayals of elite women exercising power are valid? The following comments may be helpful.

The friendship between the elder Salome and Livia, along with the broader web of relationships it spawned among the women of their families, suggests an affinity in lifestyles and mutual influence. Livia was undoubtedly

---

[23] Gundry, *Mark*, 313.
[24] Hoehner, *Herod Antipas*, 122.
[25] See above, pp. xx–xxi.

one of the most powerful women in Roman imperial history. Her methods of exercising influence and Salome's would have been similiar. Although many of the accusations of cunning, murderous manipulation lodged against Livia are probably misogynistic inventions, her many decades of influence and her extraordinary longevity argue that she indeed wielded *enormous* authority.[26] Likewise, the same must be said of Salome. Whether she really engineered all of the plots, assassinations, and executions Josephus attributes to her is doubtful, but in the totality of what he narrates about Salome one perceives a person to be reckoned with. In a recent study on Roman aristocratic women Susan Wood makes a comment about Livia that could also be applied to Salome:

> Historians . . . who were generally writing long after these women and their powerful male relatives were safely dead and their dynasties defunct, often paint a virulently hostile picture of women like Livia. . . . The truth about these women's characters probably lies at some undeterminable point between the extremes of flattering official imagery and hostile literary tradition.[27]

What was the nature of the power these women yielded? First, its exercise had to correspond to the methods used by the men around them. Since no one seriously doubts that aristocratic Roman and Herodian men resorted to trickery, plotting, assassinations, poisonings, and executions, which they extended to their family members as well as to others, it cannot be doubted that the women of these families used similar means to achieve their goals. The women had to be prepared to do so as a matter of survival, mired as they were in Roman imperial and Herodian internecine warfare. Each generation of women had to learn such survival skills from the previous.

Herodias learned to be a Herodian woman most evidently through her grandmother, Salome, and her mother, Berenice. Just as Herodias had grown up learning from them, so in Mark's tale one sees her in turn teaching female strategizing to her own daughter, Salome. With the elder Salome it is particularly evident that Herodian women could be most assertive and aggressive. As Herod's sister she was closely involved with his regime throughout his life. Herod's paranoiac suspicion of those around him re-

---

[26] Matthew Bunson, *A Dictionary of the Roman Empire* (Oxford: Oxford University Press, 1991) 242, notes: "Livia lived to be 86, having displayed a methodical and precise pursuit of power that left chroniclers such as Tacitus uneasy."

[27] Susan E. Wood, *Imperial Women. A Study in Public Images, 40 B.C.–A.D. 68* (Leiden: Brill, 1999) 5.

quired that Salome be ever on guard to protect herself and those family members in her favor.

Herodias was more than Salome's granddaughter, more than just a young Herodian female grandchild to be guided into adulthood; she stands out also as Salome's heiress apparent. Even in the meager data Josephus conveys about Herodias she is reported to have been quite aggressive, more like grandmother Salome had been than like her easily manipulated mother Berenice (at least as Josephus tells their stories). Defying the convention of her time, but determined and driven like Salome, Herodias did not shrink from actions that had public and political repercussions. She divorced her first husband and incestuously married the tetrarch of Galilee, having demanded that he divorce his Nabatean wife, thus alienating the feared Nabateans. And in the latter part of her life, yet to be discussed here, she persuaded Antipas to make a disastrous visit to the emperor.

From her grandmother and mother Herodias would have adopted various ways to defeat or obliterate any opposition she encountered. Murder was one of those techniques. Salome is alleged to have prodded Herod to carry out numerous executions, including that of her second husband, Costobarus, and Berenice's husband, Aristobulus, Herodias' father. Berenice may have colluded in her husband's death; she obviously remained on good terms with Salome following it. But if Herodias learned to live with murder as a potential way to solve problems within the family, then to use it for problem-solving regarding non-family members must have been an obvious given. To an extent, therefore, when Herodias called for the head not of a husband, but of a troublesome prophet, she was actually rather tame.

Did She or Didn't She?

The greatest obstacle to assuming that the realism of Mark 6:17-29 is historical is that Josephus never tells the same tale. This is not to override the point made earlier that his version and Mark's stand as two complementary, not contradictory perspectives on John's death. Here the point to be made is that Josephus had a penchant for giving details about Herodian women that reflect unfavorably upon them as aggressive and interfering. This is evident in his data about Herodias in other events of her life, making it inexplicable that he would not have told about her actions if she had orchestrated the Baptist's death—unless Josephus did not know that. Even with his emphasis on Antipas' political concerns as his reason for killing the Baptist it would have been like Josephus to comment that his wife had goaded him to do it.

So why did Josephus fail to tell this spicy story when he obviously had a "fondness for [recounting] the dramatic, pathetic, erotic, and the exaggerated"?[28] One explanation, in addition to a further suggestion to be made in the next chapter, concerns the Baptist. Recall that Herodias has a place in Mark's tale only because John is a key figure in his gospel. In the same way she is not in Josephus's account of John's death because John is so minor a character to him, important enough to mention to illuminate events under Antipas, but not so significant that Josephus elaborates on the details surrounding his death.

In sum I am open to, although not sure of, the general historicity of Mark 6:17-29. It appears fully possible that Herodias, with the aid of her daughter, manipulated Antipas into executing the Baptist. It makes sense that she would have used an occasion such as a feast to force a public statement from him that he would have John beheaded. It is not unimaginable that Herodias had her daughter push him to do it immediately, even as they feasted. Beyond this, however, it is also probable that oral tradition, under the influence of biblical intertextuality and other popular lore, embellished the tale, adding such details as the promise of Antipas and the platter.

"Grandmother, What Big Teeth You Had!"

To conclude to the probable historicity about Mark 6:17-29 is not novel. It is to join the majority of commentators throughout Christian history, who have blamed Herodias, as well as her daughter and Antipas, for the Baptist's death. At the same time, we have achieved this position here in a somewhat novel fashion. My openness to the historicity of Mark 6:17-29 has derived primarily from the *biography* of Herodias, that is, from the context of her life as an aristocratic Herodian woman as it was sketched in the first two chapters and will conclude in the next. Among the Herodian women and their Roman counterparts who formed the matrix of Herodias' life, and in keeping with her own character, it is quite realistic that Herodias exercised power within her family along the lines Mark describes. Viewed in the context of her own Herodian aristocracy and Roman friends, Herodias, and her daughter too, are relatively tame. After all, they only asked for the scruffy head of a poor desert preacher, a non-relative and someone far from their inner circles. Unlike some of their foremothers, neither killed any of their multiple husbands or other close family members. What would grand-

---

[28] Shaye J. D. Cohen, *Josephus in Galilee and Rome. His Vita and Development as a Historian*. CSCT 8 (Leiden: Brill, 1979) 233.

mother Salome, Berenice, Livia, and the other older ladies of the club have said about that? Perhaps that times were changing.

Mark's (Ab)Use of Herodias

The final part of our discussion about Mark and Herodias concerns the prominence he gave to her story. Beyond the obvious fact that 6:17-29 explains that Antipas had put John to death, why did Mark include the whole, very detailed story about Herodias and Salome? The point about the impact of the Baptist's death, significant as it is in Mark's theological structure, could have been made without narrating such soap-opera-like events. Luke certainly opted for a brief yet effective summary about John's death in Luke 3:19-20. Even Matthew, who kept the Markan story, nevertheless reduced its details. Also puzzling is that Mark includes the long tale in a document in which he otherwise reveals himself to be a person of brevity (in spite of a tendency also to restate the obvious).

One can only conclude that the long story of the Baptist's death served a definite purpose for Mark. In this respect Walter Wink has observed:

> What is really significant is . . . that this rambling, unedifying ac-count of John's death is included at all. After [he has telescoped] the entire ministry of John into four verses in chapter one [1:4; 7-9], Mark's leisurely narrative here is somewhat disconcerting. No doubt Mark is fascinated by the gory story. But he has a point to make. He places it after the report of Jesus' increasing popularity and success, and tells us how the report reacted on Herod's guilt for having killed John.[29]

The problem with Wink's observation, however, is that Mark's story does *not* dwell on Herod's guilt. It focuses rather on Herodias and Salome and their power over Antipas. It must therefore be assumed that the useful-ness Mark recognized in telling the story has something to do with the two women.

When compared with Matthew and Luke, Mark is amazing in his presentation. Matthew vastly tones down the revengeful Herodias, and Luke goes so far as to omit all the details of how she and her daughter negotiated John's beheading. Matthew and Luke can also be read, however, not as merely more concise but as *uncomfortable* with telling about two powerful women. In stunning contrast, Mark tells a tale in which Herodias

[29] Wink, *John the Baptist,* 11.

and Salome are prominent and very manipulative. While the two women
stand out for Mark's audience as cunning villains, one could learn from
them how to employ the same skills for the good. Readers of Mark's Gospel
who were powerless might find these women inspiring in an odd sort of
way. After all, if they could show how one seizes the moment for evil, do
they not also suggest using similar ways to accomplish good? Mark seems
unafraid of setting such female role models before his readers. While Matthew severely toned down Herodias and Luke muted her, apparently to
avoid showcasing just such paradigms of female boldness, we must ask
why Mark had no qualms in telling this story.[30]

One suggestion is that Mark wanted to use the two women against
themselves typologically, as sharp examples of "Woman as Evil" to be
wary of. Elisabeth Schüssler Fiorenza offers an analysis along these lines.[31]
In a context in which she demonstrates the use of feminist rhetoric to allow
different voices in the biblical text to speak, Schüssler Fiorenza quotes
from an essay by one of her students, Maureen Mara. She describes Mara's
paper as a "creative re-presentation [that] combines the methods of historical exegesis with creative imagination in order to recover the voice of
Herodias."[32]

Mara's text, worded as if spoken by Herodias herself, indicates that,
other than the information that accords with Josephus, either Mark's legendary sources or his own imagination wove Herodias and Salome into his
story with no historical basis for their actions. Herodias is exploited, a
woman to whom Mark affords power only in doing evil. Salome is included
only to delight the men and to help accomplish her mother's evil deed.

In Mara's view, with which Schüssler Fiorenza apparently agrees,
Herodias and Salome in the hands of Mark, or the tradition as it came to
him, were victimized by a patriarchal world and have been condemned by
Bible readers ever since for a crime they absolutely, historically did not
commit. As if Herodias herself could protest to modern female readers of
Mark's gospel, Mara has her say:

> To know me may not have been to love me, BUT
> To know me only from this biblical text is NOT to know me.
> My hope now lies in you, My Sisters—

---

[30] Note that the various theories in the following discussion differ on whether the story
is historical.

[31] Elisabeth Schüssler Fiorenza, *But She Said. Feminist Practices of Biblical Interpretation* (Boston: Beacon, 1992) 48–50.

[32] Ibid. 48.

Have courage to question
to be suspicious of biblical texts about women like me found on pages
    dubbed
GOOD NEWS and proclaimed as WORD OF GOD.
Be tenacious in your struggles to know the truth
to name the oppression where you find it
and to set free and proclaim a
LIBERATING WORD. . . .[33]

This creative reimagination of the Herodias story, in spite of the poignancy it conveys concerning the victimization of possibly innocent women, is nevertheless beset with various problems. First, while Mara rightly argues that a feminist hermeneutics of suspicion should be applied to androcentric texts, she is more suspicious of Mark than she is of Josephus. She takes Josephus as objectively authoritative and Mark or his oral sources as heavily manipulative. Yet it is quite possible that Josephus omitted from his remarks the historical role Herodias played. True, Josephus is interested in Herodias and her manipulation of Antipas elsewhere in his narratives, yet we have noted that her absence from his narrative about the death of John may reflect Josephus' lack of interest in John and is neither proof that Herodias played no role in the event nor an indication that Markan tradition invented her role.

Furthermore, Mara's assertion that Mark "pulled [Herodias] into this story from outside as the Woman to blame—the sinner—the temptress"[34] is not corroborated by the portrayal of women throughout the rest of his gospel. With the exception of Herodias and her daughter and possibly the mother of Jesus (3:31-34), all the other females in Mark are depicted positively (see, e.g., 5:21-34; 7:24-30; 14:3-9; 12:41-44; 14:66-69). Also, Mark tells about Herodias and Salome with no generalizing editorial comments. He does not warn about a link between women and evil. Rather, Mark deals with his female characters generally as individuals, good or bad, and then not necessarily with an emphasis on their gender.

It is too imaginative to assert that Mark or his oral tradition edited Herodias into the story *solely* as the archetypal evil woman. That she was powerful, manipulative, and intent on evil is, of course, clear in the text. But Mark appears mostly interested in her cleverness, her determination to take matters into her own hands and to exercise power via the only avenue open to her, familial manipulation.

[33] Ibid. 50.
[34] Ibid. 48.

A second theory concerning Mark's inclusion of 6:17-29 relates to the overall positive light in which this gospel places women (apart from the exceptions noted above). Mary Ann Tolbert observes:

> This almost universally positive portrayal stands in striking contrast to the dominantly negative portrait of the twelve male disciples in Mark. It forms the basis for the claims of many feminist scholars that the Christian community reflected by Mark's Gospel must have contained strong women leaders and role models, since the Gospel itself so clearly uses women characters in such a fashion.[35]

Correspondingly, Mark's portrayal of Herodias' power and aggressivity could bear overtones representing female leaders or role models who had been troublesome for Mark's readers. Herodias may represent for Mark not so much a woman who perpetrated evil as *a person of power* who manipulated her weak husband and naïve daughter in order to hurt the innocent. In Tolbert's view Herodias "personifies the terrible mischief routinely unleashed on the world by powerful and wicked people [of either gender]."[36] From Mark's perspective that mischief could be fomented by either women or men.

Tolbert's suggestion that Mark thought of Herodias as a person of power is engaging. I would develop her analysis in a different way, however, to more fully explain why Mark gives Herodias' story so large a portion of his text. My suggestion requires looking not so much at the women in Mark's gospel as at the women in the context to which the gospel is directed.

Accustomed to Calculating Women

If the evangelists' redaction of the material about Herodias is any indication, it appears that Mark's church, unlike those of Luke and Matthew, was not so concerned to accommodate to the social conventions of the Roman empire regarding women; Mark exhibits no need to tone down or squelch Herodias. He lets her be aggressive, manipulative, and evil, and makes no moralizing comments. One suspects, therefore, that Mark's community was more accustomed than Matthew's and Luke's to stories of powerful, interfering aristocratic females, and that Mark more than the other synoptic writers had a toleration for, even a fascination with telling such tales. Perhaps Herodias was not as culturally shocking to Mark as she apparently was to Matthew and Luke.

[35] Mary Ann Tolbert, "Mark," in Carol A. Newsom and Sharon H. Ringe, eds., *The Women's Bible Commentary* (Louisville: Westminster John Knox, 1992) 263–74, at 263.
[36] Ibid. 272.

There is reason to think that Mark's audience was used to hearing about women who exerted power via palace intrigue. He would have known that this tale of Herodias would resonate with a "fascination with royals" already developed in his readers. This is not to suggest, however, that Mark was a sensationalist, but merely that he saw in the saga about the death of the Baptist a story his readers would find intriguing. So he narrated the episode at some length.

This suggestion is based on the probability that Mark and his readers were living in Rome.[37] There stories of imperial familial intrigue were popular on the streets and in venues like the Circus Maximus and theaters, locations where the personae of the stories could occasionally be glimpsed and from which their palaces could be seen. Who in Mark's Roman church would not have heard many stories of the Julio-Claudian (e.g., Livia) and Flavian women's powerful roles? What Roman Jewish Christian was unaware of how enmeshed the Herodian aristocracy was with the imperial family? Also, if Mark's gospel is to be dated about 70, as is widely held,[38] was he not writing when Titus, emperor Vespasian's son, had just returned to Rome from the Jewish war with his Herodian mistress Berenice? With even the Roman Senate publicly known to be infuriated by her presence, what stories did Berenice's appearance cause to be circulated in Rome? And what tales about other women in her family, such as about her aunt Herodias and cousin Salome, did talk about Berenice generate, especially among the Christians like Mark?

The theory of Roman provenance for Mark's gospel has not gone unchallenged, however. A strong case has also been argued, for example, for Mark having written in and for a Syrian readership.[39] Without reconstructing the debate here, and although I find the Roman theory more compelling, even if the provenance was Syria my suggestion that Mark was responding to his readers' "royal" interests in telling the Herodias tale remains applicable. The history of Herod the Great's huge family is replete with Syrian contacts. This includes the fact that Herodias' daughter, Salome, had been the Queen of Chalcis and that her brother, Agrippa I, had been closely involved over some years with Flaccus, the Roman proconsul of the province. If Mark was writing in Syria he could have been aware of local curiosity about the aristocracy, especially stories involving Herodians.

---

[37] Others have fully summarized the data connecting Mark with Rome. See Marcus, *Mark 1–8*, 30–33 (although this author does not link Mark with Rome himself).

[38] See Marcus, *Mark 1–8*, 37–39 for an overview of the arguments.

[39] So Marcus, *Mark 1–8*, 33–37.

Mark's inclusion of the Herodias tale in no way signals his approval of her actions. What he may have actually thought of her as a powerful female is hard to gauge. If his gospel is a document written in Rome for the church there, however, one can note that the limited emancipation of Roman women, while partially supported by legislation, was accepted only with enormous difficulty. The attitude of some men toward women who used their liberties is reflected in, for example, the famous sixth *Satire* of Juvenal (ca. 55–128 C.E.).

> Whatever the tragic poets
> Tell us about Medea and Procne may well have happened:
> I won't dispute that. Such women were monsters of daring
> In their own day—but not from lust for cash.
> We find it less freakish when wrath provides the incentive
> For a woman's crimes, when whitehot passion whirls her
> Headlong, like some boulder that's carried away by a landslide.
> What I can't stand is the calculating woman
> Who plans her crimes in cold blood. Our wives sit and watch
> Alcestis undertaking to die in her husband's stead:
> If they had a similar chance, they'd gladly sacrifice
> Their husband's life for their lapdogs'. (642-50)[40]

While this passage probably postdates the writing of Mark's gospel by a decade or more, one can wonder whether Mark had any sympathies with this mentality. If so, would he have thought of Herodias as one of Juvenal's "less freakish" women, since her crime was due to whitehot passion? Or would Mark have seen her as "calculating," the type of woman most abhorrent to Juvenal? It is impossible to tell if Mark had been acculturated into such extreme misogynism. But did later Christians who read Juvenal as well as Mark's gospel think of Herodias when they read Juvenal's text?

A String of Insults

> *"Herodias watched and delighted to see the passions of her sensual*
> *husband moved at sight of her daughter's charms, to hear the rash*
> *promise from those unrighteous lips. Base were the means,*

---

[40] As cited and translated in Eva Cantarella, *Pandora's Daughters. The Role and Status of Women in Greek and Roman Antiquity* (Baltimore: Johns Hopkins University Press, 1987) 147.

*and baser still the end. When woman's charms are used not only to
provoke lust, but to induce cruelty, can there be a more awful
instance of the misuse of the fair gifts of the Creator?
Yet history tells of many a tale like this, though perhaps of
none so utterly and so irredeemably mournful."* [41]

In his famous London stage play the British actor Alec McCowen
gives a solo performance of the King James Version of Mark.[42] Though
McCowen claims his rendition is verbatim, that he adds not even one additional word to the *KJV* translation, nevertheless with skillful inflection he
does apply his own twentieth-century redaction. In repeatedly calling
Herodias "Herodi-ASS," McCowen creates a demeaning pun in contemporary English, where previously Herodias' Idumean Jewish Hellenistic
name bore no play on words.

This is but one of the more recent in a long string of insults directed at
her throughout the history of Christianity. Whether or not she was historically guilty of the death of a prophet, she has certainly been unremittingly,
verbally stoned to death for it ever since (notably at the hands of preachers
as mirrored in our quotations). Throughout the centuries, while some may
have assumed that Mark's story is legendary and that Herodias and Salome
were really not guilty, there is no reflection on how that would have been
an injustice done to the two women. Only in the writings of recent feminist
commentators has this latter issue even been raised.

It would be interesting to conclude my feminist discussion of this tale
with a verdict of "not guilty as charged" and "victimized by misogynistic
imagination." But even feminist studies are hardly predisposed to finding
only perfect women, and that is certainly not where this investigation has
led. I think it very possible that Herodias and Salome indeed goaded
Antipas into executing John. At the same time, these Herodian women and
their crime must be evaluated within their broader contexts, as this book
has attempted to do. Herodias played the paranoid, aristocratic family
game she was born into brutally well, outsmarting the fox who held his
patriarchal upper hand over her, forcing him to stamp out the voice that had
criticized them both. And in Salome she passed on her "wisdom" to the
next generation of females. Herodias won in a power game where all lives,
including her own, were quite cheap.

---

[41] H.D.M. Spence and Joseph Exell, eds., *The Pulpit Commentary: The Gospel according to Mark* (Chicago: Wilcox and Follett, 1909) 253.

[42] Alec McCowen, *St. Mark's Gospel* (video recording) (New York: Arthur Cantor Films,
1990).

Integral to feminism is the search to uncover the historical truth about patriarchy and the limitations it has placed on women. Herodias is an example of a woman, extraordinarily privileged in the context of her day yet unable to lash out satisfactorily, in her own estimation, against the criticism of a male prophet who castigated her and her husband for their marriage. Nor could she could easily overthrow the power of her husband who had placed the prophet in protective arrest. Driven by her own sense of revenge, she fell back on her matriarchal training.

CHAPTER SEVEN

Life After the Banquet

*"Whether or not there be any truth in the tradition that Herod threw
the head over the walls of the black fortress of Machaerus . . . we
may be certain that his cruel paramour, when she had once got into
her possession her strange plaything, on its golden charger, would
never think of gratifying his disciples by giving it to them for decent
burial. So that we may, with perfect certainty, conclude, in thinking
of that funeral somewhere among the lonely wilds, on the eastern
side of the Dead Sea, that it was a mutilated corpse that these men
took up. . . . But we can well believe . . . that noble head was ever
present to their mind's eye, with the flowing locks that had never
been cut, with its tongue that had never faltered in its holy message,
and its eyes that had never flinched before tyrant mob or tyrant king."* [1]

To be left holding John's head on a platter may have cast Herodias in a
triumphant stance. But there are some prizes one does not want to keep. This
haughty winner certainly did not go off to bury John's head herself. That she
physically disposed of it by her own hands is possible, however. One could
toss an object from the stronghold of Machaerus' steep perch and it would
move easily into a fast tumble far into deep ravines below. John's mouth, as if
its silence was not enough, would have been mutilated beyond recognition.

Even though Mark's Christian readers would no doubt have believed
that people who go bowling with prophets' heads ultimately receive their
due, he neither moralizes for them about Herodias and Salome nor does he
tell anything further about them. The rest of their story had nothing to do
with the rest of his. Mark does say more about Antipas. He indicates that
the tetrarch was haunted by his killing of John and wondered if Jesus was

---

[1] John H. Burn, *A Homiletical Commentary on the Gospel according to St. Mark*
(London: Funk and Wagnalls, 1896) 215–16.

John *redivivus* (6:16). Luke also gives a bit more information about Antipas, to which we now turn.

Making New Friends

To learn about Herodias, Salome, and Antipas after John's beheading (ca. 28 C.E.) we rely primarily upon Josephus, and for one event on Luke. The Third Gospel has a tradition, not found elsewhere, that Antipas interrogated Jesus during his final days (Luke 23:7-12). Luke says that Antipas was in Jerusalem when Jesus was arrested (ca. 30 C.E.). Antipas, and presumably Herodias, had gone there most probably for the Passover. Pilate was also in the city for the feast. When informed that Jesus was a Galilean, and thus under the tetrarch's jurisdiction, he sent Jesus to Antipas. While the tetrarch questioned Jesus, he received no answers. Luke reports that Antipas and his soldiers mocked Jesus and sent him back to Pilate. Then Luke comments: "That same day Herod and Pilate became friends with each other; before this they had been enemies" (23:12). In Luke's narrative Pilate states that he and Antipas concurred that Jesus was not guilty of any of the charges against him (23:14-15).

Luke gives no indication whether Herodias had any involvement in these proceedings. Matthew may indirectly offer a bit of insight, however. While he does not tell about Antipas interviewing Jesus, he does have Pilate's wife in mind in his Passion narrative and, as noted earlier, Matthew appears to have paralleled her with Herodias and her intervention against the Baptist. Is the choice of the two women mere coincidence, or was Matthew aware that they, like their husbands, had been at odds?

Marriage to an Old Uncle

> *"Give a daughter in marriage, and you complete a great task;*
> *but give her to a sensible man."*
>
> (Sir 7:25)

To weave into this what happened to Salome after dancing at Machaerus it is necessary to recall details about her earliest years. We must also attempt to more closely gauge her birth date, which falls sometime between 3 and 20.[2] Salome's birth to Herodias and her first husband, Herod II, probably took place in Azotus, Ascalon, or Caesarea. She bore the name of two powerful

---

[2] See above, p. 15 concerning the marriage date of Herodias and Herod II. Nikos Kokkinos, "Which Salome Did Aristobulus Marry?" *Palestine Exploration Quarterly* 118

and well-known foremothers, her great-grandmother and her more remote ancestor, the Hasmonean queen Salome (Shelamzion) Alexandra. She would have been given other names also, perhaps including that of her mother, Herodias.

Salome was first married to her uncle Philip, her father's half-brother. Philip was also the half-brother of Herodias' father, thus Salome's great uncle on her mother's side. A son of Herod the Great by Cleopatra of Jerusalem, Philip was born ca. 20 B.C.E. He had spent some of his youth in Rome and had been in and out of favor with his father. Under the final settlement of Herod's will Augustus made Philip tetrarch of Batanaea, Trachonitis, Auranitis, Gaulanitis, and portions of what had been called the "domain of Zenodorus" in the region of Panias.

It is unknown whether Philip, who was between two and four decades older than Salome, had been married previously. It is clear that he and Salome were childless and that he had no other children (*Ant.* 18.137). Depending upon what year her birth date fell between 3 and 20, Salome could have married Philip no earlier than 15 and no later than 33.

The tetrarchy that Philip ruled from 4 B.C.E. to 34 C.E. was populated mainly by Gentiles. This freed the Herodians there of many of the difficulties Philip's half-brothers and their wives, Antipas and Herodias, Archelaus and Glaphyra, faced regarding the religious susceptibilities of their Jewish subjects. It also allowed Philip to produce coins bearing portraits, notably of Augustus and Tiberius.[3] Philip enlarged the city of Panias as his capital, calling it Caesarea in honor of the emperor. It came to be known as Caesarea Philippi. He also transformed a fishing village on the north shore of the Sea of Galilee, Bethsaida, into the city of Julias, naming it after Augustus' daughter, Julia Major. This change must have taken place early in Philip's rule, before 2 B.C.E. when the disgraced Julia was exiled.

Philip died in 34 C.E. at his winter palace in Bethsaida Julias. Tiberius took over his territory and annexed it to the province of Syria. Josephus summarizes Philip's rule in glowing terms:

> In his conduct of the government he showed a moderate and easy-going disposition. Indeed, he spent all his time in the territory subject to him. When he went on circuit he had only a few select companions. The throne on which he sat when he gave judgment accompanied him wherever he went. And so, whenever anyone appealed to him for redress

---

(1986) 33–50, at 39, places the marriage of Herodias and Herod in 2 B.C.E. and thus the birth of Salome in 1 B.C.E. His forced dating, however, functions to make it impossible that she could have been the wife of her second husband, Aristobulus.

[3] See David Braund, "Philip," *ABD* 5:310–11, at 311.

along the route, at once without a moment's delay the throne was set
up wherever it might be. He took his seat and gave a hearing. He fixed
penalties for those who were convicted and released those who had
been unjustly accused. (*Ant.* 18.106-108)

We have only our imagination to help us factor Salome into this idealized
picture. After Philip's death Salome's life took an interesting turn. She became what her mother, with the greatest of effort, never achieved: Salome
became a queen.

Marriage to a Young Cousin

Sometime after 34 C.E. Salome married her first cousin, Aristobulus,
prince of Chalcis. He was the son of Herodias' brother Herod, King of
Chalcis, and his first wife, Mariamme. It is difficult to estimate Aristobulus'
age. He was born in 12 or 13 C.E. at the earliest. Josephus refers to him as
"Aristobulus the Younger" (*Ant.* 20.13). In the light of much other information in Josephus, however, there are questions about the birthdate of this
Aristobulus, resulting in uncertainty about whether Salome really could
have been his wife. We will return to this discussion, noting for now that
according to Josephus Salome had three sons by Aristobulus: Herod,
Agrippa, and Aristobulus.

A Trip to the Olympics?

Some think that Antipas and Herodias were traveling abroad in the
period just after Philip's death in 34. There are two Greek inscriptions, one
on the island of Cos (*OGIS* I, 416) and one on Delos (*OGIS* I, 417), that
have suggested this theory. Dedicated to the honor of Antipas, and using
his title of "tetrarch," they were commissioned, respectively, by a certain
Philo and by the Athenian people.[4] Each was apparently occasioned by a
visit from Antipas. Attempts have been made to correlate them with the
three trips Antipas is known to have made to or from Rome as tetrarch: his
return to Galilee and Peraea from Rome in 4 B.C.E., his journey to and from
Rome following the visit to Herodias and her first husband when she
agreed to marry him, and his final journey to Rome, accompanied by
Herodias, in 39.

It has also been suggested, however, that the inscriptions came from a
trip following Philip's death in 34, even though Antipas is not said to have

---

[4] See David C. Braund, "Herod Antipas," *ABD* 3:160.

made a journey then. This assumes that Antipas would have gone to Rome, urged on by Herodias as happened later in 39, to ask to govern the regions annexed to Syria after Philip's death.[5] Since 33/34 C.E. was the year of the 203rd Olympiad this theory would also explain Antipas' visit to Greece.[6] But nothing in Josephus supports a journey by Antipas to ask for Philip's territories. Furthermore, the later trip in 39, which Josephus does recount, would hardly have taken place if Antipas and Herodias had only a few years before been to Rome with an unsuccessful bid. As engaging as it is to think of the royal pair stopping off at the games, a trip by Antipas and Herodias to Rome following Philip's death is unlikely given their subsequent actions. Could one suspect, then, that they made a trip to Greece just for the Olympics, and thus the inscriptions? That would be a mere guess. It is best to assume that the two texts honoring Antipas were composed in relation to journeys he is certain to have made.

Dinner on the Euphrates

While nothing confirms that Herodias might have gone to the Olympics, the probability is strong that she traveled with Antipas far to the northeast and was present for a magnificent banquet he held in the middle of the Euphrates. This occurred during negotiations between the Romans and the Parthians in 36. That was a busy year for the Roman governor of Syria, Lucius Vitellius, who had entered office in 35 C.E. In 36 he removed Pontius Pilate from office, sending him to Rome to report to Tiberius, and also deposed Joseph Caiaphas from the high priesthood. Meanwhile Tiberius instructed Vitellius to negotiate a treaty of friendship with Artabanus, king of the Parthians. Artabanus was at the time hostile toward Tiberius because of the emperor's attempts to unseat him.

Vitellius and Artabanus agreed to meet at the border between Syria and Parthia, on the Euphrates, in the middle of a bridge, each with his own bodyguard. These treaty negotiations turned out to be successful, and were sealed by handing over hostages, including Artabanus' son who was to be sent on to Tiberius. Antipas and an entourage probably including Herodias were present at these negotiations, although his role is not clear. Possibly he acted as a broker between Vitellius and Artabanus. In any case, Josephus says that once the terms of the treaty had been agreed upon "Herod the tetrarch gave a feast for them in a luxurious pavilion he constructed in the middle of the river" (*Ant.* 18.102).

[5] So Kokkinos, "Which Salome," 40.
[6] Ibid.

Was this structure on the bridge or on a sandbar? The elegant scene can only be imagined. And where should one picture Herodias and the other women of the various delegations at the feast? Were they in the midst of things or gathered at some distance on the riverbanks? Were the women watching the female slaves dancing for the men under the stars? Would Herodias have thought back on another banquet some eight years earlier, a night when the dancer was her young daughter? She had brokered the negotiations herself then, and a head had rolled. When she remembered John's death, *if* she thought back on him, what did she feel? Triumph or relief? Had she any shred of remorse, or any regrets about how she had silenced him? No one knows what this complex woman might have thought as the Euphrates, like the mighty waters of time, swept past.

The Revenge of the Nabateans

Antipas may have helped Vitellius obtain a treaty with the Parthians, but he did not remain in the good graces of the Syrian legate for long. Viewing the success as a way to increase his standing with Tiberius, Antipas quickly communicated the news about the hostages to the emperor. Nevertheless he "wrote and dispatched by couriers so precise and complete an account that he left nothing for the proconsul [Vitellius] to report" (*Ant.* 18.104). When Vitellius was eventually informed by the emperor that Antipas had reported the facts first "Vitellius fell into a great fury, and took the offence to be greater than it actually was" (*Ant.* 18.105). Josephus says that he kept his wrath concealed, however, until, after Gaius became emperor, he was able to get even.

Meanwhile, revenge was being heaped upon Antipas from another source. It came from his former father-in-law, Aretas I, who had long held a grudge against the tetrarch for divorcing his daughter (in ca. 23). While she had cleverly managed to escape to Nabatea before Antipas could banish her, the woman's father had yet to avenge her. It seems unusual that Aretas had waited a decade or more for the right opportunity, yet this appears to be what happened. Aretas and Antipas had also been involved in a dispute about boundaries in the district of Gabalis. All of this came to a head in 36 and a battle ensued in which "the whole army of Herod [Antipas] was destroyed . . ." (*Ant.* 18.113).

The defeated Antipas sent word to Tiberius, who became infuriated at Aretas for initiating hostilities against another Roman client. Tiberius ordered Vitellius to declare war upon Aretas and to bring him to Rome in chains or send his head. Vitellius pushed toward Petra, but part way there he, Antipas, and some friends "went up to Jerusalem to sacrifice to God during the traditional festival the Jews were celebrating there" (*Ant.* 18.122), i.e., the Passover of 37. During those few days in Jerusalem Vitellius was notified of the death of Tiberius and the accession of Gaius. Vitellius then cancelled his army's advance toward Nabatea.

Antipas thus stood not only defeated but without his Roman patron to punish his opponent. Even from his own subjects he did not receive full support. Josephus reports that there were Jews who viewed the destruction of his army as "divine vengeance, and certainly a just vengeance, for his treatment of John, surnamed the Baptist" (*Ant.* 18.116). It was this statement by Josephus that occasioned his long flashback telling the circumstances under which Antipas put John to death. As if defeat by an enemy and approval of it by some of his own subjects were not enough, however, Antipas, and particularly Herodias, also received news in 37 that was especially disheartening to them.

Brother Agrippa's Unwelcome Ascent

With the death of Tiberius in March 37 the fortunes of Herodias' brother, Agrippa I, and his wife Cypros took a rapid turn for the better. Herodias' jealousy over this set the scene for a dramatic turn of events in her own life. In 36 Agrippa had gone to Rome. Josephus (*JW* 2.178) says that he went to Tiberius "to accuse Herod the tetrarch," although no indication is given of what he intended to say. Since Antipas was by then fighting with Aretas, Agrippa's accusation may have related to those events, although his greater purpose in visiting the emperor may have been to request the deceased Philip's domain for himself.

Agrippa, via Cypros, as we already saw, had borrowed funds for the trip and to pay off old loans in Rome. Upon satisfying his debt to the imperial treasury he was reinstated in his friendship with Tiberius. The emperor then appointed him to be the companion of his grandson, Tiberius Gemellus. Agrippa also became friends with the latter's rival, Gaius, better known as Caligula. Agrippa went so far in currying favor with Gaius that it got him into serious trouble. Agrippa's chariot driver overheard him saying to Gaius that Tiberius ought to relinquish his office to him since Gaius was the more capable of ruling. After the driver reported this to Tiberius, Agrippa was cast into prison. He remained incarcerated until Tiberius died six months later.

As soon as Gaius became emperor he freed Agrippa and made him king over what had been the old tetrarchy of Philip and the more northerly tetrarchy of Lysanias.[7] Agrippa waited until the second year of the reign of Gaius, thus between March 38 and March 39, before leaving Rome to secure his rule. Josephus reports that upon his arrival in Palestine Herodias was thunderstruck.

> Herodias . . . begrudged her brother his rise to power far above the state that her husband enjoyed. Agrippa had had to flee for lack of money to pay his debts, but now he had returned in grandeur and with such great prosperity. It was consequently painful and depressing for her to see so great a reversal in his fortunes. The spectacle of his royal visits in the customary regalia before the multitudes made her especially helpless to keep the unfortunate envy to herself. (*Ant.* 18.240-41)

As Daniel Schwartz comments, "Those who had supported the impoverished Agrippa and insulted him on this background as well, and probably suffered insults in return, were now forced to see the upstart as a king and imperial favorite, and it must have hurt."[8] With Agrippa's appointment, Cypros became a queen. This, too, must have galled Herodias, who had once helped her save her spendthrift husband from suicide. The status and future wealth of the children of Agrippa I and Cypros, Agrippa II, Drusus, Berenice, Mariamme, and Drusilla was now elevated as well.

To Be or Not to Be a Second Fiddle?

". . . It is heartache and sorrow
when a wife is jealous of a rival. . . ."

(Sir 26:6)

Herodias insisted that Antipas should go to Rome and sue for equal status with Agrippa.

> For their life was unbearable, she said, if Agrippa, who was the son of that Aristobulus [i.e., her own father] who had been condemned to death by his father, who had himself known such helpless poverty that the necessities of daily life had entirely failed him, and who had set out on his voyage to escape from his creditors, should have returned as a king, while Herod [Antipas] himself, the son of a king, who was called by his royal birth to claim equal treatment, should rest content to live as a commoner to the end of his life. (*Ant.* 18.242-43)

---

[7] Later, upon the death of Gaius in January of 41, Agrippa also became king of Judea.

[8] Daniel R. Schwartz, *Agrippa I. The Last King of Judea.* Texte und Studien zum Antiken Judentum 23 (Tübingen: Mohr, 1990) 56.

This, of course, is Josephus' summary of what he attributes to Herodias. It would be ironic if she had actually argued that that her Idumean/ Samaritan husband, Antipas, even though a son of Herod the Great, had a greater *claim* to royalty than her brother with whom she shared Hasmonean blood. An argument that Josephus neglects to put in Herodias' mouth, but that must have been a cogent one, was that Antipas had already ruled loyally and successfully for Rome for more than thirty years and surely deserved a promotion before the spendthrift Agrippa. Josephus reports that Herodias also admonished Antipas:

> "Even if, O Herod . . . you were not distressed in the past to be lower in rank than the father from whom you sprang, now at last I beg of you to move in quest of the high position that you were born to. Do not patiently admit defeat by a man outranking you, who has bent the knee to your affluence. Do not inform the world that his poverty can make better use of manly qualities than our riches. Never regard it as anything but a disgrace to play second fiddle to those who were but yesterday dependent on your bounty for survival. Come, let us go to Rome; let us spare neither pains nor expense of silver and gold, since there is no better use for them than to expend them on the acquisition of a kingdom." (*Ant.* 18.243-44)

With these words Herodias expresses what must have been a much observed point about Agrippa's accession: He had spent borrowed sums lavishly on currying favor with Gaius. If that paid off for him, could not the wealthy Antipas and Herodias also be elevated through similar gift-giving?

Hounding the Fox

"A headstrong wife is regarded as a dog. . . ."

(Sir 26:25)

Josephus says that Antipas resisted Herodias' pressure for a while, content with his tranquility and not attracted by Rome. But Herodias urgently insisted that he should seek a throne at any cost. Herodias "never flagged till she carried the day and made him her unwilling partisan, for there was no way of escape once she had cast her vote on this matter" (*Ant.* 18.245).

In this one hears echoes of Herodias' grandmother Salome, who in Antipas' younger years had pushed him into going to Rome to contest Herod the Great's will. Now, some four decades later, it was Herodias who goaded Antipas to demand promotion. Antipas was probably reluctant to try again for the title he had failed to receive in 4 B.C.E. Maybe he also thought it futile to try since the new emperor was the proven friend of Agrippa.

Herodias, however, like her grandmother and her mother, may have been relying upon the friendship of imperial women for help, although it is unlikely she had any female friends left in Rome. Her grandmother's powerful patron, Livia, had died in 29, and her mother's friend, Antonia, the grandmother of Caligula, who had helped Agrippa and who might have been expected to assist another of Berenice's children, had died in 37. Antonia's daughter, Livia Julia (Livilla), a contemporary of Herodias, was also dead. It is possible that Herodias thought to establish a link with Livilla's daughter, Julia (d. 43 C.E.), but she was a minor figure in the reign of Gaius.

Other contemporaries of Herodias from her earlier Roman period to whom she might have turned for help would have been Julia Minor and Agrippina the Elder. Julia, however, had died in exile in 28, and Agrippina, the mother of Gaius, expired in 33. Of Agrippina's nine children, three daughters received much attention during their brother Gaius' reign. These women, Julia Drusilla, Julia Livilla, and Agrippina the Younger, were the powerful females whose friendship Herodias would have known to cultivate. By the time Herodias set out in 39, however, Julia Drusilla, who had achieved great prominence when Gaius first became emperor, had just died (38). Julia Livilla and Agrippina the Younger, although the latter would eventually become one of the most powerful women of her time, were not in Gaius' favor when Herodias needed their patronage. In fact, in the same year that Herodias and Antipas set off for Rome, Gaius exiled these two sisters to the Pontian islands. This speculation about women in the imperial family with whom Herodias might have established patronage bonds could be expanded, but in the end it did not matter. For once Herodias disembarked in Italy she never had time to make new friends in high places. Her brother Agrippa took care of that.

Sailing into the Sunset

> *"A sandy ascent for the feet of the aged—*
> *such is a garrulous wife to a quiet husband."*

(Sir 25:20)

Herodias and Antipas left for Rome probably in 39, most likely in the summer, "supplied as lavishly as possible and sparing no expense" (*Ant.*

18.246). They must have been heavily laden with gifts for Gaius and his entourage. When Agrippa learned of their plans he determined to turn Gaius against them. To do this he sent his freedman, Fortunatus,[9] in a ship that departed shortly after that of Herodias and Antipas. Fortunatus carried letters to the emperor denouncing Antipas. Due to a favorable voyage he was able to arrive in Campania at the same time as Antipas and Herodias.

Both parties disembarked at the port of Dicaearchia (Puteoli), Campania's central port and a major entrepôt for Rome. It is unlikely that Antipas and Herodias went from the boat immediately to see the emperor at his residence in Baiae, a few miles away. Gaius would have had numerous foreign deputations trying to see him, and Antipas and Herodias would first have entered into the social life of that hot springs resort while waiting for an audience.[10] The pair were probably unaware that they were in a race with Agrippa's freedman.

At their eventual meeting with Gaius the emperor was perusing the letters sent by Agrippa even as he was greeting them. The letters indicted Antipas for conspiring against the previous government of Tiberius. Agrippa also accused Antipas of having enough equipment for 70,000 heavy-armed foot-soldiers stored in his armories, and wrote that he intended to use this force in league with the Parthian king, Artabanus, against Gaius.

It is doubtful that Gaius was interested in the first charge since it had to do with his predecessor's administration. Josephus mentions only that he interrogated Antipas "whether the report about the arms was true" (*Ant.* 18.251). When Antipas admitted that the weapons were there Gaius regarded "the accusations of revolt as confirmed" (*Ant.* 18.252). It is not

---

[9] According to *JW* 2.183 Agrippa himself followed Antipas and Herodias to see Gaius. On this contradiction see Schwartz, *Agrippa I*, 4–5.

[10] Baiae was an opulent scene with numerous holiday villas, the ultimate resort for the aristocracy of Rome. On a beautiful bay near present-day Pozzuoli and Naples, Baiae was in the center of the most extensive region for thermo-mineral bathing in antiquity. The scene of extensive volcanic activity, this area was called the Phlegraean Fields, the "fields devoured by fire." The homes of the Roman elite were built along the water. Gaius staged a spectacle there in about 39 C.E., perhaps concurrent with the time Herodias and Antipas were present. "He collected all available merchant ships and anchored them in two lines, close together, the whole way from Baiae to the mole at Puteoli, a distance of a little more than three Roman miles. Then he had the ships boarded over, with earth heaped on the planks, and made a kind of Appian way along which he trotted back and forth for two consecutive days" (Suetonius, *Gaius* 19). He also organized processions and games that thousands watched from the hills around the bay. One theory about why Gaius bridged the bay was that an astrologer had said that he had "no more chance of becoming emperor than of riding a horse dry-shod across the Gulf of Baiae" (Suetonius, *Gaius* 19).

certain what lay behind this situation. Antipas may have stockpiled the weapons not against Gaius, but in case of more conflicts with regional leaders like Aretas IV, whom he had just fought in 36.

Agrippa would hardly have lodged a charge that was groundless. He may have gathered information about the armories of Antipas when he worked for him in Tiberias. This may have been the accusation Agrippa had intended to lay before Tiberius earlier, in 36. In the interim Antipas, aware of the friendship that had blossomed between Gaius and Agrippa, and perhaps fearing for his future in the Roman government after Agrippa was named king, could have entered a pact with the Parthians and continued to stockpile resources.[11] Whatever the real situation, Antipas did not deny the existence of the arms. Gaius consequently deprived him of his tetrarchy. Galilee and Peraea were added to Agrippa's territories. Gaius also ordered Antipas to give his own property to Agrippa. Then he condemned Antipas to "perpetual exile" (*Ant.* 18.252).

This punishment, which implies the loss of Roman citizenship for Antipas, suggests that Gaius sentenced him for treason, a crime normally punishable by death. Nevertheless *deportatio,* "deportation" was substituted because the notion of executing one of their members was offensive to the upper class. This was the most severe form of *relegatio,* "banishment" from Roman territory administered by Roman law.

Whither Thou Goest

On learning that Herodias was Agrippa's sister Gaius said she could retain her personal wealth and live under her brother's protection. Whether the emperor expected her to return to Judea or live in Rome is not evident. Gaius told her "to regard her brother as the bulwark who had protected her from sharing her husband's fate" (*Ant.* 18.253). It seems odd that Gaius was unaware of the relationship between Agrippa and Herodias, given his friendship with Agrippa. Perhaps in earlier years Agrippa had conveyed more strongly to Gaius his resentment at the condescension he had experienced from Antipas and Herodias than his blood relationship with the pair. Or perhaps Gaius feigned ignorance that Herodias was Agrippa's sister in order to belittle her. Whatever the explanation, Herodias rejected the offer to live under her brother's custody. According to Josephus she replied: "'Indeed, O emperor, these are generous words and such as befit your high office, but loyalty to my husband is a bar to my enjoyment of your kind

---

[11] Harold W. Hoehner, *Herod Antipas.* MSSNTS 17 (Cambridge: Cambridge University Press, 1972) 261.

gift, for it is not right when I have shared in his prosperity that I should abandon him when he has been brought to this pass'" (*Ant.* 18.254). Angered at her pride, Gaius exiled her also and gave her possessions along with those of Antipas to Agrippa.

Josephus concludes his narration of this event with misogynistic moralizing: "And so God visited this punishment on Herodias for her envy of her brother and on Herod for listening to a woman's frivolous chatter" (*Ant.* 18.255). In a sentimental assessment, Grace Macurdy responds to Josephus:

> One would rather say that Herodias' final renunciation of the wealth and luxury she loved and her loyalty to her old husband in the exile and disgrace she brought upon him weigh heavily in the scale against the cruelty and vanity of early deeds that are recorded against her [i.e., in the NT]. . . . Whatever the fact may be [regarding her role in the death of the Baptist], it is true that she was a fierce and luxury-loving woman, who in the end loved another human being better than herself and was willing to forego for his sake all her old vanities.[12]

Despite romanticizing Herodias, Macurdy may be somewhat accurate. Mary Lefkowitz has noted epitaph and inscriptional evidence that reflects a self-sacrificing character on the part of numerous wives in the Roman empire who decided, despite many hardships, to go into exile with their husbands.[13] On the other hand, some wives also stayed behind in order to obtain financial support for their husbands. What seems most likely is that Herodias was terrified of Agrippa's revenge and the life she would have if she were indebted to him. Therefore she opted for the safer of her choices. Furthermore, exile did not necessarily signal the end of a relatively good life for Herodias.

Josephus' moralizing, with its sweeping generalization about women's frivolous chatter, underscores our suspicions about his objectivity regarding Herodias. That his portrayal of her is highly editorialized is evident. One wonders if Herodias is not overdrawn as a manipulator in the whole story of her trip with Antipas to Gaius. Should Antipas' fall be so exclusively charged to her vices? As Schwartz has observed, "it is difficult to know where to draw the line between history and novel here."[14]

---

[12] Grace H. Macurdy, *Vassal-Queens and Some Contemporary Women in the Roman Empire* (Baltimore: Johns Hopkins University Press, 1937) 82.

[13] Mary Lefkowitz, "Wives and Husbands," *Greece and Rome* 30 (1983) 31–47, at 42–43.

[14] Schwartz, *Agrippa I*, 56.

Go West Old Man, Go West

> *"We took our fill of the paths of lawlessness and destruction,*
> *and we journeyed through trackless deserts,*
> *but the way of the Lord we have not known.*
> *What has our arrogance profited us?*
> *And what good has our boasted wealth brought us?"*
>
> (Wis 5:7-8)

Josephus states that Gaius exiled Antipas to *Lougdounon polin tēs Gallias,* i.e. "Lugdunum, a city of Gaul" (*Ant.* 18.252). This would normally refer to Lugdunum, the major city in Gallia Lugdunensis, now Lyons in France. Herodias may have been aware that this was the place of exile when she chose to go with Antipas. If so, she knew it was a flourishing Roman colony where life even for an exile might not be so bad. Lugdunum as their place of banishment, however, is challenged by a parallel passage Josephus wrote earlier, stating that Gaius ordered Antipas to go to Spain and that he "died in Spain, whither his wife had accompanied him into exile" (*JW* 2.183).

To accommodate both readings it is often suggested that the banishment was actually to a location on the frontier, Lugdunum Convenarum (now Saint-Bertrand de Comminges), a town in the Pyrenees in Gaul on the right bank of the Garonne. Schwartz, who holds that Josephus drew his information in both of these passages from the same source, offers two other explanations. He suggests that perhaps Josephus' source mentioned Lugdunum and Josephus in *JW* 2.183 thought the reference was to Lugdunum Convenarum on the Spanish border but later, by the time he wrote *Ant.* 18.252, he had learned that Lyons of Gaul was meant. Or it may be that the source explicitly referred to Lugdunum Convenarum, and Josephus, who first thought that border city was in Spain, later decided to assign it across the river Garonne to Gaul.[15]

David Braund suggests another reading to satisfy both texts. He notes that Antipas' brother, Archelaus, many years earlier had been consigned by Augustus to Vienna, a city in Gallia Narbonensis on the east bank of the Rhone, modern Vienne, France (*JW* 2.111). This was just south of Lugdunum in Gallia Lugdunensis, i.e., Lyons. Braund argues:

> . . . "Lugdunum in Gaul," unless otherwise qualified, can only mean Lyons. Further, Lyons seems attractive on other grounds. First, Antipas' detention there would neatly balance that of Archelaus at Vienne, its neighbour and rival. Second, Antipas was despatched in summer A.D.

---

[15] Ibid. 5.

39: in the autumn of that year Gaius set out for Lyons—coincidence? Third, compared with the other provincial cities used as places of detention, Lugdunum Convenarum stands out as relatively insignificant in this period: Lyons looks much more like the others. Given all this, it seems best to take the abbreviated [*JW*'s] statement to be an error, perhaps textual. Alternatively, Antipas may have left Lyons for Spain and died there: if so, there would be no contradiction in Josephus.[16]

Wherever the place of exile, the forfeiture of their property must have severely affected the lifestyle of Herodias and Antipas. However, rulers deported by the Romans were, for the most part, "detained in relatively comfortable conditions and were allowed access to the local elite at their place of detention and even contacts with their land of origin."[17] If Antipas and Herodias were indeed in Lyons, perhaps Archelaus and Glaphyra, of a comparable age but exiled to nearby Vienne more than thirty years before, became their social companions.[18] While years earlier Antipas and Herodias might have thought of the other couple as their predecessors in the political quagmire created by an incestuous marriage, they had now become also their forerunners in survival on the Rhone.

The statement in *JW* 2.183 that "Herod died in Spain, whither his wife had accompanied him" indicates that Antipas died in exile, wherever that was. While Herodias probably died in their place of banishment as well, Josephus does not say. In 39 as they journeyed to their western quarters Antipas would have been about sixty years old and Herodias would have been in her fifties. Did they outlive Gaius, who himself died in 41, and Agrippa I, who died in 44? If by any chance Herodias survived them all, might she have found a way to overturn her status of perpetual exile and return to the east to end her days? If so, her destination would probably have been the kingdom of Chalcis, where her daughter, Salome, was living with her husband, Aristobulus, and their three sons.

The Royal Women of Chalcis

Turning our attention now to Salome, we note that in 44 C.E. Salome's father-in-law, Herod the king of Chalcis, married as his second wife his

---

[16] David Braund, *Rome and the Friendly King* (London: Croom Helm, 1984) 177 n. 76.
[17] Ibid. 173.
[18] The dream of Glaphyra (see above, p. 46) may suggest that she died shortly before or after the exile began in 6 C.E. See David Braund, "Archelaus," *ABD* 1:367–68, at 367, who notes that while Archelaus is presumed to have died in Vienne his tomb was later pointed out to visitors to Bethlehem, according to Jerome.

niece, Berenice, daughter of Agrippa I and Cypros. Before his death in 48 Herod had two sons by Berenice, Berenicianus and Hyrcanus. When he died his kingdom was given by the then emperor, Claudius, not to his older son Aristobulus, Salome's husband, but to Berenice's brother, Agrippa II, who then ruled it from 48–52. After 48 the widowed Berenice lived many years with Agrippa II (incestuously, it was rumored), presumably remaining in Chalcis during his administration.

This data suggests that beginning in 44 and for some years thereafter Berenice and Salome, who were first cousins and married respectively to father and son, must often have been together. This ought not to be overlooked, given the subsequent life of Berenice and the role she may have played as one of Josephus' direct sources in Rome.

The Age Factor

In 52 Salome's husband, Aristobulus, was finally given his father's kingdom by the Romans. Claudius had taken it away from Agrippa II after allotting him other territories. The fact that Chalcis had not been given to Aristobulus in 48 is interpreted by some as an indication that he was too young at the time. Nikos Kokkinos argues that confirmation of this is found in a reference by Josephus to him, in a text regarding events in 45, as *Aristoboulō tō neōterō* (*Ant.* 20.13). Kokkinos reads this phrase to indicate that Aristobulus was Herod's "young" son in 45, and thus not ready to be appointed ruler of Chalcis three years later when his father died.[19]

If it were true that Aristobulus was not mature enough to rule in 48, then he could hardly have been married to Salome in 34. This would raise problems concerning the historicity of their marriage, as indeed is Kokkinos's point. He thinks that Aristobulus was married to some other Salome. However, Kokkinos' argument hinges on his unusual reading of *Aristoboulō tō neōterō* as effectively meaning "the young Aristobulus." A translation of the phrase as "Aristobulus the Younger" is more accurate. This implies that Aristobulus was *relatively* younger than another person of the same name whom Josephus had in mind, i.e., either his father's brother or their very famous father, also Herodias' father. Josephus had used similar phrasing just before, in *Ant.* 20.9, referring to *hō neōteros Agrippas,* "the younger Agrippa," in a relative sense.

The argument that Aristobulus was too young in 48 to be given Chalcis overlooks other factors in the context. Most discussions of this situation fail to consider the presence of women and therefore give no attention to

---

[19] So Kokkinos, "Which Salome," 35.

Berenice. Yet she is probably the major reason why her brother, Agrippa II, and not her son-in-law, Aristobulus, was given the territory. Before Herod of Chalcis' death Agrippa II was in Rome at the court of Claudius. Claudius wanted to give him Agrippa I's kingdom when he died in 44. He was advised against that because of Agrippa II's youth (he was born in 28), but the chance to appoint him to Chalcis in 48 was an opportunity Claudius must have welcomed. At the same time Berenice may have sensed her husband's impending demise and hence may have warned Agrippa to petition Claudius to give Chalcis to him rather than to Aristobulus. This worked out in Berenice's best interest, as perhaps she had foreseen, since she became Agrippa's consort in Chalcis.

Berenice's manipulation of the succession in Chalcis is so obvious an explanation of why Aristobulus was sidetracked that one wonders why it has not been suggested before. Yet in this and many of the discussions concerning Herodian history scholars often overlook the role of women unless Josephus or some other ancient author has expressly mentioned them. When Berenice is part of a scenario, however, she must be given serious attention, for if Herodias and her grandmother, Salome, left a legacy of determination to any woman of their family in the mid- and late first century, Berenice was surely the person. But hers is another whole story that takes us far afield. We return now to her cousin, Salome.

There is no compelling reason to think Josephus was wrong, *contra* Kokkinos, when he stated that Aristobulus married Salome upon Philip's death (*Ant.* 18.137). Aristobulus' birth was in 12 or 13 C.E. at the earliest and Salome's was between 3 and 20 C.E. The latter span allows that Salome may have been a bit older than her second husband, but because she gave birth to three children by Aristobulus after 34 it seems more probable that she was born closer to the end of this period. Moreover, *if* one views her dance leading to John's death in 28 as erotic, that would argue that she must have been born at least a few years before 20 in order to make her about 11 or 12 in 28. Thus she may have been born about 16 and have been a few years younger than Aristobulus. In any case there remains no serious reason to doubt that her second marriage was to Aristobulus of Chalcis.

Queen Salome

Following Aristobulus' appointment in 52 as King of Chalcis, the emperor Nero in 54 made him King of Armenia Minor as well. From this period there is a bronze coin[20] minted in the eighth year of the reign of

---

[20] Concerning the various specimens of this coin see ibid. 47 n. 1.

Aristobulus; reckoning from his appointment in 54, this dates it from 62.[21] It bears likenesses of both Aristobulus and Salome. On the obverse is the portrait of Aristobulus and the words "King Aristobulus." Salome is on the reverse, which reads "Queen Salome."[22] Her stylized face has simple and severe lines. While one interpretation is that she is wearing a crown in the form of a hat,[23] the more common explanation is that her hair is arranged in small braids all over her head, held in place by a narrow band, with long braids hanging down below her neck.[24] Macurdy commented that this portrait of Salome "shows her as a middle-aged woman with long, intelligent features. . . ."[25] What intelligent features might be, however, is debatable. Furthermore, how close this portrait is to the real Salome cannot be known.

Whether Salome is wearing a hat or a band, she is not veiled. Like this coin, various contemporaneous mosaics also show women with their faces and hair uncovered. But there is also evidence that some women in the eastern regions of the Roman empire used veils. Salome's uncovered hair not only allowed her stylishness to be displayed but also reflects the influence of the cosmopolitan aristocratic circles within which she lived. As Ramsay MacMullen has observed:

> Women who imitated the changes in style that went on at the imperial court, changes depicted in the provinces by portraits of the ladies of the imperial house, were the richer ones, the more open to new ways, and the more likely to belong to families on the rise. Women of the humbler class went veiled, but these others behaved exactly like their counterparts observed in Italy, fully visible, indeed making their existence felt very fully in public.[26]

On the basis of the numismatic evidence Salome must have died after 62, since she appears on the coin from that year with her husband, but

---

[21] So Ya'akov Meshorer, *Ancient Jewish Coinage. Vol. II: Herod the Great through Bar Cochba* (Dix Hills, N.Y.: Amphora Books, 1982) 171. Cf. Kokkinos, "Which Salome," 47 n. 1, who disputes Meshorer's reading of the date and places it about 69/70 C.E.

[22] See Meshorer, *Coinage,* 280 and plate 29 for pictures of the coin; it was cast in bronze with all inscriptions in Greek.

[23] So Tal Ilan, *Jewish Women in Greco-Roman Palestine: An Inquiry into Image and Status* (Peabody, Mass.: Hendrikson, 1995) 132 n. 20.

[24] So Macurdy, *Vassal-Queens,* 83; Kokkinos, "Which Salome," 34.

[25] Macurdy, *Vassal-Queens,* 83.

[26] Ramsay MacMullen, "Women in Public in the Roman Empire," *Historia* (Wiesbaden) 29 (1980) 208–18, at 217–18.

Aristobulus alone is found on the next one he is known to have minted, cast in 71.[27] How long Aristobulus outlived Salome is uncertain.

Encircled by a Growing Movement

Salome probably outlived her mother. Whether they ever saw one another after Herodias and Antipas left for Rome to ask Gaius to elevate their status is not known. If they were even friendly cannot be ascertained. Nor is there any hint whether Salome or her mother had lived with any regrets about their lives, especially concerning the death of the Baptist. Undoubtedly they could not have forgotten the incident, since the preaching about the resurrection of Jesus and his messiahship, along with the interpretation of John as his forerunner, spread throughout their domains from the 30s on. The Herodian family could not have isolated themselves from discussion about these developments. Even some of their employees joined the followers of Jesus. For example, one member of Antipas' court, his childhood companion Manaen, by the mid-40s was a significant member in the church of Antioch (Acts 13:1). Manaen may have left Antipas' entourage when it was dissolved by his exile in 39, or he may have gone to Syria earlier if his beliefs made him unwelcome in palace circles. And even as Herodias and Antipas shipped off to Rome in 39 one suspects that talk of Jesus was occurring in ports like Caesarea and on the boats in which they sailed. The presence of the royal pair on the sea routes would have reminded the storytellers of the Jesus movement to recount Jesus' run-ins with "that fox" and to tell how John was beheaded because of his wife. Maybe many stares and whispers accompanied the royal duo on their long journey to Italy.

A few years later Herodias' brother, Agrippa I, would also use imprisonment and execution in dealing with various figures associated with Jesus. Just before his own sudden death in 44, having been "eaten by worms" (Acts 12:23), Agrippa persecuted James and Peter. He ordered James "killed with the sword" (Act 12:1-2), although whether this means by piercing or beheading is not said. Then he had Peter imprisoned and bound with two chains (Acts 12:3-19). When Peter escaped, Agrippa retaliated against the prison guards by ordering their death.

By the late 50s, however, the interface between the Herodians and the Christians had really changed, at least as Luke tells the story. When Agrippa I's children, Berenice, Agrippa II, and Drusilla had encounters

---

[27] See Meshorer, *Coinage*, 2:280.

with Paul their judgments about him were quite neutral; they seem not to have considered ordering his death (Acts 24:24-26; 26:31).

Queens, Kings, and Pawns: Same Game, Different Strategies

These observations suggest that while the generations of Herodians such as Antipas, Herodias, and Agrippa I, who dealt with the initial figures associated with Christianity, used death to wipe out the figures they perceived as problematic, the later Herodians were more reserved in their judgments. This parallels something we have noted with respect to the Herodian women. Herodias' grandmother Salome, to the extent Josephus can be believed, had family members killed or collaborated in their annihilation when it served her needs. Her daughter Berenice seems to have assented to her mother's actions since they apparently remained on good terms; Berenice herself, however, is not said to have murdered close relatives. In the same way her daughter, Herodias, who called for the execution of a personally troublesome prophet, is not reported to have solved *familial* problems by murder. Herodias' daughter, Salome, who functioned as her pawn in achieving the prophet's death, likewise is not said to have killed any relatives. "Death as solution" *within* the family seems to have been on the decrease among the Herodians. What seems not to have waned as later generations of Herodians dominated the stage, however, was the determination of some women to steer the course of their own lives as had Herodias and her grandmother Salome. The torchbearer of their spirit for the latter half of the first century was Berenice.

Berenice's Men

Berenice's fascinating story is, unfortunately, too long to be told in full here. Having already noted a few details about her, we will pick up the thread of her life in the period of the Jewish War (66–70). By that time Berenice (b. 28) had been married three times, widowed twice, and divorced once. Through her (second) marriage to Herod of Chalcis she had become a queen and was accorded that title from 44 on. From 48 on, except for a very brief marriage to Polemo of Cilicia, Berenice had lived with Agrippa II, first in Chalcis and then in various other territories he governed.

Berenice was rich in her own right, perhaps due to wealth she had amassed in Chalcis. This came into play during the Jewish War in which she and Agrippa, who had tried unsuccessfully to intercede on behalf of the

Jews and prevent the war, nevertheless sided with the Romans after it began. In 68, with the war still raging, the Roman general Vespasian left for Rome to become emperor. Berenice is said to have contributed to the financing of his successful power bid. At the same time she became the mistress of Vespasian's son, Titus, who headed the Roman forces in Judea. Ten years her junior, Titus was said to have been charmed by her (Tacitus, *History* 2.2). One summary of Titus and his activities at the end of the war sketches this picture:

> After addressing his troops, awarding honors, offering sacrifices and feasting with his troops, Titus entrusted the custody of the area to the tenth legion, dismissed the twelfth to service on the Euphrates, and took the fifth and fifteenth with himself to Caesarea on the coast. . . . Since it was now October and not a time to sail for Italy, Titus cavorted for a time with Agrippa in Caesarea Philippi and presumably with the Jewish king's sister Berenice, who had taken a strong liking to Vespasian and had a passion for Titus. . . .
>
> In Caesarea Philippi, Titus, using his Jewish captives, put on all kinds of spectacles, beastly shows, and gladiatorial contests. . . . From a certain perspective it was an incongruous, incredible time. A Jewish king was entertaining the conqueror of his fellow religionists while enjoying shows produced by the further decimation of Jewish flesh. While Jerusalem's ashes still smoldered, the passion of an uncircumcised future Roman emperor burned for one of the last of the Hasmonean beauties.[28]

When Titus left Judea ca. 71 for Rome Berenice did not go with him. She arrived four years later, accompanied by Agrippa. The delay may have been caused by senatorial controversy, since Titus's liaison with Berenice, and the rumor that she was going to marry him, were scandalous to the Romans. They would generally not have approved at that time of marriage between an emperor and a woman from the provinces. Once in Rome, however, Berenice lived with Titus and occasionally acted publicly as his wife.

In 79 Vespasian died and Titus became emperor. Berenice then expected to become empress. Due to public reaction, however, Titus was forced to send her away (Dio Cassius, *Hist.* 65.15). Suetonius comments that Titus was "naturally kind-hearted" (*Titus* 8) and therefore his banishment of Berenice "was painful for both of them" (*Titus* 7). It appears,

---

[28] John H. Hayes and Sara R. Mandell, *The Jewish People in Classical Antiquity* (Louisville: Westminster John Knox, 1998) 203–204.

based on a statement by Dio Cassius (*Hist.* 66.18.1), that she returned to Rome in 81 just before Titus died, and apparently then remained in the city without further scandal.

Edited in Rome

The years between 75 and 79, and from 81 on, when Berenice and Agrippa were intermittently in Rome, coincide with Josephus' postwar life there. The latter was writing and would publish the first six books of *The Jewish War* in about 79, with the seventh and final book coming at the end of the century, just before his death (ca. 100). Josephus was no doubt gathering material for *Antiquities* (finished ca. 90) at the time Berenice and Agrippa lived in the imperial city. He states that Agrippa was a major source of information for him (*Life* 362-66; *Apion* 1.51). He also says he consulted with "certain of his [Agrippa's] relatives" (*Life* 363). Berenice was surely one of those people.

The witness of Agrippa and Berenice to Josephus is confirmed particularly in Books 18 and 19 of *Antiquities,* which highlight the role of Agrippa I. Who better than two of his children to supply details about their father's life? This does not imply, however, that Josephus was so friendly with Agrippa II and Berenice that he did not dispute their perspectives. It is interesting to observe that Agrippa I is portrayed more positively on the whole by Josephus in *Antiquities* than are Agrippa II and Berenice. Several of the unfavorable statements about the two are found in *Ant.* 20 (e.g., 20.145-46). This suggests that Agrippa II must have died before or while *Ant.* 20 was being written. This is not certain, however, since Josephus insists that he was unafraid to offend the living. In *Ant.* 16.187 he states that, while he had respect for many of Herod the Great's descendants who were still reigning, "we have honoured the truth more than them, and on some occasions, indeed, when this was rightly done, it provoked those very persons to anger."

Discussing Berenice as a source for Josephus raises the fascinating issue of the extent to which her female perspective colored his narration of events. And since Berenice probably had more interest in telling about the women of her family than Agrippa did, is Berenice perhaps the real explanation for the striking omission we have been dealing with throughout this book, Josephus' non-inclusion of Herodias' role in his information about John's death? Was John's death, from Berenice's perspective, and Agrippa's as well, a minor incident in the lore about the women of their family? Also, the fact that Berenice had lived with Salome for four years in Chalcis raises the issue of what version of the story she knew. Had Salome minimized the tale over the years as she lived with her role as pawn and murderess? What version did she tell Berenice? Furthermore, was Berenice, as Agrippa I's daughter, perhaps unsympathetic toward her aunt Herodias, the sister Agrippa I greatly disliked? While one might argue that was a reason for Berenice to have told Josephus the worst of stories about Herodias, maybe it was more likely the cause for her to say very little.

These musings about what Berenice's attitude was are merely that: musings. They suggest, however, that in the perspective Berenice and Agrippa had on their family's history the murder of a prophet by Herodias and Salome may not have been very significant. Why bother to highlight the story of how their aunt had gotten rid of a troublesome marginal character? If Josephus knew the tale from other sources they may even have told him it was blown out of proportion.

Other people, however, did go out of their way to pass on the story of Herodias and the Baptist, and around 70 C.E. it was written into a document that has come to be called the Gospel of Mark. For the author of that gospel and his readers, in *their* "family" history the evil deed wrought by Herodias and Salome was a pivotal, decisive event. It was the martyrdom of a great prophet and foreshadowed what would happen to their beloved leader, Jesus. What Herodias and Salome did to the Baptist thus was preserved not by the Herodian family nor their countryman, Josephus, for whom it may not have seemed worth remembering, but by the dead prophet's friends—for whom it was appalling.

EPILOGUE

Life After Death

> *"There is no venom worse than a snake's venom,*
> *and no anger worse than a woman's wrath."*
>
> (Sir 25:15)

For the past two thousand years Herodias and her dancing daughter have lived vividly in the histories of earliest Christianity. Because Mark wrote the story of how they killed the Baptist into his gospel, and then Matthew edited a version of it into his, these two women and that fox they manipulated are solidly enshrined among the Bible's evildoers. For biblical readers, however, what frustration there has been in reading so powerful a tale yet having no source to supply missing details, no full-blown narrative of subsequent events, and no thorough analysis of motives. This, like many biblical stories, has left readers hungering to know more. If only the gospel writers, and Josephus, too, had written fuller accounts. . . .

The Stuff of Legends

> *"The end of an unrighteous generation is grievous."*
>
> (Wis 3:19)

The demand for more information led very early to the development of Christian legends by those only too glad to supply the rest of the story. They especially told how Herodias and Salome were punished. A detailed, comprehensive survey of this legendary material is available in a large, profusely illustrated work, *Great Women of the Bible in Art and Literature.*[1]

---

[1] Dorothée Sölle, Joe H. Kirchberger, and Herbert Haag, *Great Women of the Bible in Art and Literature* (Grand Rapids: Eerdmans, 1994) 252–61.

Here, just to cite a brief example, we note that in Syrian legend Herodias' real name is Polia, and she has John tortured in a fortress called Machaea near the Dead Sea. When her daughter, Boziya, is given the head of John on a platter she takes it first to her mother and then to a frozen pond upon which she dances with it. But the ice breaks and swallows her up so that no one could save her. The tetrarch then has the daughter beheaded with the very sword that killed John. When her head is taken to her mother on a silver platter the mother goes blind. When she reaches out to touch John's head in hope of a cure her hand withers; when she tries to cry out her tongue is split. She ends up possessed by the devil, and must be tied up, the rest of her life spent in misery. In other similar narratives when the daughter falls through the ice it cuts her head off.

Slavonic Josephus

Besides inspiring legends, the Gospel tale of Herodias and Salome had an impact on subsequent versions of *The Jewish War*. As we have observed, when Josephus reported in *Ant.* 18:116-19 that Antipas killed John as a preemptive measure because he feared the Baptist would lead an uprising, he said nothing about the prophet criticizing Antipas' marital escapades or anything about Herodias' role in his death. That material is found only in the gospel texts. There are, however, various medieval (approximately eleventh-century) manuscripts of *The Jewish War* that give more data about John than Josephus did in *Ant.* 18:116-19 and that generally harmonize with the gospels' information, including some reference to Herodias and Antipas. These manuscripts are called the Old Slavonic version although they are actually written in Old Russian.

An example of such data is a passage in the Slavonic manuscripts after *JW* 2.168. It follows upon information Josephus gave about the governing of their tetrarchies by Antipas and his brother Philip:

> Philip, during his government, saw a dream, to wit that an eagle plucked out both his eyes; and he called all his wise men together. When some explained the dream in this manner and others in that, there came to him suddenly, without being called, that man of whom we have previously written, that he went about in animals' hair and cleansed the people in the waters of the Jordan. And he spake: "Hear the word of the Lord— the dream that thou hast seen. The eagle is thy venality, for that bird is violent and rapacious. And this sin will take away thine eyes, which are thy dominion and thy wife." And when he had thus spoken, Philip expired before evening, and his dominion was given to Agrippa.

And his wife [Herodias] was taken by Herod [Antipas] his brother. Because of her all law-abiding people abhorred him, but durst not accuse (him) to his face. But only this man, whom we called a savage, came to him in wrath and spake: "Forasmuch as thou hast taken thy brother's wife, thou transgressor of the law, even as thy brother has died a merciless death, so wilt thou too be cut off by the heavenly sickle. For the divine decree will not be silenced, but will destroy thee through evil afflictions in other lands; because thou dost not raise up seed unto thy brother, but gratifies (thy) fleshly lusts and committest adultery, seeing that he has left four children." But Herod, when he heard (that) was wroth and commanded that they should beat him and drive him out. But he incessantly accused Herod, wherever he found him, until he (Herod) grew furious, and gave orders to slay him.[2]

Scholarship widely judges this passage to be a medieval interpolation into the text. It obviously has drawn upon the gospel material about Herodias, especially Mark, where she is incorrectly named as Philip's wife, and also appears influenced by legends of the type described above.

The Psychoanalysis of Herodias and Salome

Much of the literature, art, drama, and opera concerned with Herodias and Salome from the late medieval period to the present[3] does not so much contrive additional events to connect with the two women, but analyzes their motives in bringing about John's death. The overriding question that drives much of this material is: Whence the viciousness toward John of both Herodias and Salome? The consistent answer in these sources is that only the Baptist's rejection of the love of either Herodias or Salome for him could explain their desire for blood revenge.

A classic example reflecting this type of analysis is Richard Strauss' 1905 opera *Salome,* based on the drama of the same title written by Oscar Wilde in 1893. In this opera, which is widely performed internationally, it is supposed that Salome had fallen in love with the Baptist but he had rejected her advances. In revenge Salome, wielding power over Herod by her erotic dancing, persuades him to order the death of the Baptist, whose severed head she then is able to kiss despite his rejection.

---

[2] This translation by Henry St. John Thackeray is found in the appendix of the principal additional passages in the Slavonic Version in the LCL Vol. 3 of Josephus, 646–47.

[3] See the comprehensive overview in Sölle et al., *Great Women,* 258–62.

In the End: Death to a Righteous Man

> *". . . those that seek my soul, to destroy it,*
> *shall go into the lower parts of the earth.*
> *They shall fall by the sword: **they** shall be a portion for foxes."*

(Psalm 63:9-10 KJV)[4]

Did Herodias and Salome care about, even hate or love their victim, John the Baptist, as some have suggested? That remains unknowable to us. What we have seen clearly is that the two women were playing a power game they had learned from the family and social circles that had mentored them. Herodias and Salome had pitted themselves against a foxy old king to make him use his power as they wished. When they maneuvered him into checkmate, he was forced to do their bidding—and an innocent, courageous, powerful, yet humble man was executed. This was a crass and dangerous game, especially if you were the pawn, a mere honest prophet. Herodias and Salome were brilliant players, and they won their game resoundingly. The prophet's friends and followers, then and now, however, would argue that one ought never to be deceived by apparent victories in the name of evil.

---

[4] Boldface added.

A P P E N D I X   A

The Family of Herodias
(partial chart)*

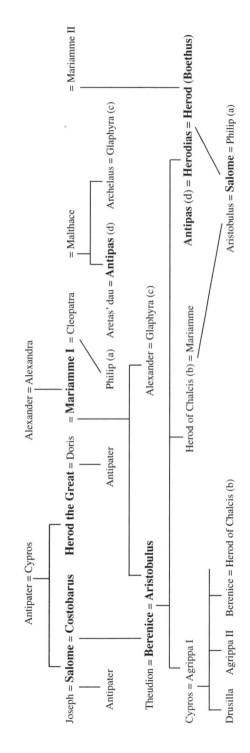

* Corresponding letters in parentheses denote identical individuals.

Synoptic Table

Matthew 14:3-12	Mark 6:17-29	Luke 3:19-20
		19 But Herod the ruler [Gk. tetrarch], who had been rebuked by him because of Herodias, his brother's wife, and because of all the evil things that Herod had done, 20 added to them all by shutting up John in prison.
3 For Herod had arrested John, bound him, and put him in prison on account of Herodias, his brother Philip's wife,	17 For Herod himself had sent men who arrested John, bound him, and put him in prison on account of Herodias, his brother Philip's wife, because Herod had married her.	
4 because John had been telling him, "It is not lawful for you to have her."	18 For John had been telling Herod, "It is not lawful for you to have your brother's wife."	
5 Though Herod wanted to put him to death, he feared the crowd, because they regarded him as a prophet.	19 And Herodias had a grudge against him, and wanted to kill him. But she could not, 20 for Herod feared John, knowing that he was a righteous and holy man, and he protected him. When he heard him, he was greatly perplexed; and yet he liked to listen to him. 21 But an opportunity came when Herod on his birthday gave a banquet for his courtiers and officers and for the leaders of Galilee.	
6 But when Herod's birthday came,		

the daughter of Herodias danced before the company, and she pleased Herod 7 so much that he promised on oath to grant her whatever she might ask.

8 Prompted by her mother,

she said,

"Give me the head of John the Baptist here on a platter." 9 The king was grieved, yet out of regard for his oaths and for the guests,

he commanded it to be given; 10 he sent and had John beheaded in the prison. 11 The head was brought on a platter and given to the girl, who brought it to her mother. 12 His disciples came and took the body and buried it; then they went and told Jesus.

---

22 When his daughter Herodias came in and danced, she pleased Herod and his guests; and the king said to the girl, "Ask me for whatever you wish, and I will give it." 23 And he solemnly swore to her, "Whatever you ask me, I will give you, even half of my kingdom." 24 She went out and said to her mother, "What should I ask for?" She replied, "The head of John the baptizer." 25 Immediately she rushed back to the king and requested, "I want you to give me at once the head of John the Baptist on a platter." 26 The king was deeply grieved; yet out of regard for his oaths and for the guests, he did not want to refuse her. 27 Immediately the king sent a soldier of the guard with orders to bring John's head. He went and beheaded him in the prison, 28 brought his head on a platter, and gave it to the girl. Then the girl gave it to her mother. 29 When his disciples heard about it, they came and took his body, and laid it in a tomb.

APPENDIX C

Chronology [1]

B.C.E.	29	Execution of Mariamme I
	28	Execution of Costobarus, second husband of Salome
	23	Birth of Herod II (Boethus), first husband of Herodias
	20	Birth of Antipas, second husband of Herodias
	17	Marriage of Aristobulus and Berenice, parents of Herodias
between 16 and 12		Births of Herodias, Mariamme, and Herod of Chalcis (order uncertain)
	10	Birth of Agrippa I
	7	Execution of Aristobulus, father of Herodias
between 7 and 4		Agrippa I and Berenice move to Rome
between 7 and 6		Birth of Jesus
	6	Betrothals of Herod of Chalcis, Herodias, and Mariamme
	4	Execution of Antipater
		Death of Herod the Great
		Salome and her family, including Herodias, move to Rome

[1] Most of these dates are approximate. The years given for the birth, ministry, and death of Jesus as well as the beheading of John the Baptist rest on the argumentation of John P. Meier, *A Marginal Jew. Rethinking the Historical Jesus. Vol. I: The Roots of the Problem and the Person* (New York: Doubleday, 1991) 372–409.

C.E. between 1 and 2	Herodias returns to Judea; marriage to Herod II (Boethus)
between 3 and 20	Birth of Salome, daughter of Herodias and Herod II (Boethus)
between 9 and 12	Death of Salome, grandmother of Herodias
between 21 and 23	Visit by Antipas to Herodias and Herod II on way to Rome
23	Divorce of Antipas and his Nabatean wife
	Marriage of Antipas and Herodias
	Death of Berenice, mother of Herodias
24	Agrippa I returns from Rome to Judea; employed by Antipas
26–36	Pontius Pilate procurator of Judea
28	Birth of Berenice, daughter of Agrippa I
	Beheading of John the Baptist
	Beginning of the public ministry of Jesus
30	Crucifixion of Jesus
34	Death of Philip, husband of Salome, daughter of Herodias
	Marriage of Salome to Aristobulus of Chalcis
36	Defeat of Antipas by Aretas IV
36	Agrippa I in Rome; imprisoned six months
37	Death of Tiberius; Gaius Caligula becomes emperor
	Agrippa I made King over northern territories of Philip and Lysanias
37	Birth of Josephus
38	Return of Agrippa I from Rome to Judea
39	Herodias and Antipas journey to Rome
	Banishment of Herodias and Antipas to Lugdunum
41	Death of Gaius Caligula
	Agrippa I becomes King of Judea

between 41 and 44	Agrippa I persecutes Peter and executes James the son of Zebedee
between 43 and 44	Death of Agrippa I
44	Marriage of Berenice to Herod of Chalcis
50	Death of Herod of Chalcis
	Agrippa II is given kingdom of Herod of Chalcis
between 62 and 71	Death of Salome, daughter of Herodias
70	Gospel of Mark
79	Publication of *Jewish War* 1–6 (Book 7 ca. 100)
85	Gospel of Matthew
85–90	Gospel of Luke
89	Publication of *Antiquities*